Joseph W. Miller

The American supplement to the Synopsis

Joseph W. Miller

The American supplement to the Synopsis

ISBN/EAN: 9783337140038

Printed in Europe, USA, Canada, Australia, Japan

Cover: Foto ©Suzi / pixelio.de

More available books at **www.hansebooks.com**

THE AMERICAN

SUPPLEMENT TO THE "SYNOPSIS,"

CONTAINING

American Inventions in the Chess Openings;

TOGETHER WITH

FRESH ANALYSES IN THE OPENINGS, SINCE 1882.

EDITED BY

J. W. MILLER,

EDITORIAL STAFF OF THE CINCINNATI COMMERCIAL GAZETTE.

LONDON:

W. W. MORGAN JUN., 17 MEDINA ROAD, HOLLOWAY, N.

SIMPKIN, MARSHALL AND Co., STATIONERS' HALL COURT, E.C.

AUG. SIEGLE, 30 LIME STREET, E.C.

1885.

CONTENTS.

————:o:————

INTRODUCTION.

—:0:—

FEW words are needed in introducing the "American Supplement to the 'Synopsis'" to English Chess Players,—its republication in this country is at once a testimony to its value, and a return of the compliment paid by the Americans to the last edition of the "Synopsis;" with this important difference,—that whereas the Americans took the 140 pages of the "Synopsis" without one word of acknowledgment, the editor of this reprint fully recognises his indebtedness to Mr. Miller, and those who assisted in the compilation of the "Supplement." This may be but scant repayment for the labour entailed, but it is better than none at all. Perhaps, in years to come, when the law of International Copyright has been amended, such compliments as this will be neither necessary nor possible, but as the matter stands at present we hold that acknowledgment should be inseparable from copying, and we are pleased to say this rule is pretty generally recognised. Mr. Miller's neglect of it, therefore, is all the more noticeable, and has induced us to refer to it. With these few words we let the "American Supplement to the 'Synopsis'" speak for itself.

PREFACE.

— :o: —

THE Editor does not assume to be an analyst of Chess apart from the army of Chess players who have given thought and study to the Openings, and played them for many years. The body of analysis in the German Handbuch is the product of ten thousand minds; and the best analysts have not been infallible, as witness the declaration of Howard Staunton that the Sicilian was the best Opening for the second player. The Chess Openings come and go out of fashion without much regard for individual preferences; and they stand on shifting ground, sometimes strengthened temporarily by a new line of play, and again laid on the shelf as the novelty is fully dissected and its weak points made known. It is certainly desirable to put on record all noteworthy ideas in the Openings; and this is the aim of the Editor, especially for those originating on this side of the Atlantic. Space will also be given to the freshest foreign analysis. Nearly three years have elapsed since the third edition of Cook's " Synopsis " was published. Since its appearance there have been memorable International Chess Congresses in London, Vienna, and Nuremberg, and several Chess matches between the great Masters. The proof reading has been carefully supervised, the Editor regarding this as one of the vital things in the publication of these works. His warm thanks are due to many American lovers of Chess for valuable suggestions and assistance in collecting material.

EXPLANATION OF NOTATION AND TABLE OF ABBREVIATIONS.

BLACK.

QRsq / QR8	QKtsq / QKt8	QBsq / QB8	Qsq / Q8	Ksq / K8	KBsq / KB8	KKtsq / KKt8	Ksq / KR8
QR2 / QR7	QKt2 / QKt7	QB2 / QB7	Q2 / Q7	K2 / K7	KB2 / KB7	KKt2 / KKt7	KR2 / KR7
QR3 / QR6	QKt3 / QKt6	QB3 / QB6	Q3 / Q6	K3 / K6	KB3 / KB6	KKt3 / KKt6	KR3 / KR6
QR4 / QR5	QKt4 / QKt5	QB4 / B5	Q4 / Q5	K4 / K5	KB4 / KB5	KKt4 / KKt5	KR4 / KR5
QR5 / QR4	QKt5 / QKt4	QB5 / QB4	Q5 / Q4	K5 / K4	KB5 / KB4	KKt5 / KKt4	KR5 / KR4
QR6 / QR3	QKt6 / QKt3	QB6 / QB3	Q6 / Q3	K6 / K3	KB6 / KB3	KKt6 / KKt3	KR6 / KR3
QR7 / QR2	QKt7 / QKt2	QB7 / QB2	Q7 / Q2	K7 / K2	KB7 / KB2	KKt7 / KKt2	KR7 / KR2
QR8 / QRsq	QKt8 / QKtsq	QB8 / QBsq	Q8 / Qsq	K8 / Ksq	KB8 / KBsq	KKt8 / KKtsq	KR8 / KRsq

WHITE.

PLAN OF THE WORK.

The tables are so arranged that each column contains the moves of a single variation. The moves are expressed as fractions; the move of the first player, whom we invariably call White, being above the line, and the move of the second player, Black, below.

The notation is the most concise English method in use at present, and will be easily understood by the reader.

ABBREVIATIONS.

K stands for King or King's

Q „ „ Queen or Queen's

R „ „ Rook or Rook's

B „ „ Bishop or Bishop's

Kt „ „ Knight or Knight's

P „ „ Pawn or Pawn's

+ „ „ superior position or game (if above the line for White, if below the line for Black).

ch stands for check

sq „ „ square

x „ „ takes

en pas „ „ en passant

= „ „ even game

! „ „ best move

? „ „ weak move

The figures at the top of the tables are the numbers of the columns, inserted for reference.

The numbers in the margin indicate the order in which the moves are to be played.

RECENT PRACTICE IN THE OPENINGS OF THE BEST PLAYERS.

IT may be taken for granted that the Chess Master never reveals his opinion of the various Openings so unmistakably as when he meets other Chess Kings over the board in the International Chess Congresses. He will skirmish and experiment in off-hand play, and give much attention to the hazardous moves of current analysis in the periodical press, but when confronting another player of the highest ability he becomes conservative, and his Chess, in the Openings at least, takes a narrower range. In the International Tournaments at Vienna, 1873, and Paris, 1878, the Gambits were neglected, not one game in ten being a Gambit. In the International Tournament Paris, 1878, four Gambits were declined and accepted in one hundred and two games. As the late Mr. John Wisker said in 1880 : " The present generation of Chess-players seem to have convinced themselves that serious games are not to be won by tripping up the adversary in the Opening, but by sound calculation and judgment in the middle of the game, and accurate play at the end. We do not regret the change. It puts an end to Gambit-mongering—to getting an Opening by rote, and playing it off against an unwary adversary—and brings the functions of the Chess-player to their legitimate bearings. Chess under the Congress system is likely to become more a matter of science, and less a thing of quips and cranks than it has been heretofore. As to ' lively chess ' we hold the opinion that the Openings without sacrifices present abundant scope for brilliant combinations. It must be remembered, moreover, that five-sixths of the lively games recorded in print have arisen from weak moves by players innocent of great intricacies."

In August, 1882, Mr. G. Reichhelm, of Philadelphia, one of the veteran analysts of the United States, wrote, in answer to a correspondent's question : " Are Gambits sound ?" that " the theoretical verdict is constantly changing. In the Muzio, Allgaier, Kieseritzky, and Evans Gambit the defence is at present considered to have the best of it, the strong point against the Evans being the so-called Compromised Defence. The Ruy Lopez Opening is the strongest *debut* in which no sacrifice is made, but all the Gambits are practically sound, for the attack generally wins two-thirds of the games."

The Vienna International Tournament, in the summer of 1882, lasted for over a month. We find but two Gambits (Evans and Allgaier) in the collection of forty-two games of that Congress published by Mr. A. G. Sellman, of Baltimore. The London Congress of 1883 was the greatest of Chess gatherings in its proportions and duration. Mr. Thomas Long, the distinguished analyst, after summerizing the Openings at the Congress, reaches the following conclusions :

1. That the Regular Openings, as against the Irregular, are the favourites by upwards of 3 to 1.

2. That amongst the Regular Openings the open games predominate by about 100 to 80 over the close ones.

3. That the open Regular, the Ruy Lopez, is first favourite, by a small majority, over the first close Regular, the French, viz., as 53 to 49.

4. That in the Ruy Lopez, **the** favourite defence is 3 P-QR3, **by 27 to 19, 4 and 3 respectively.**

5. That different players adopt various moves at the same stage in the same Opening.

6. That the same players also adopt different moves at the same stage in the same Opening.

7. That Chess practice shows that at almost every step in each variation of all the Openings there are several roads equally safe, and that, according to **the** temperament of the player at the time, or in accordance with his ordinary style of play, will such and such a move be selected.

8. That the best players at times adopt moves—even in important Tourneys —which they condemn, as is evidenced in several of the late Congress games.

9. That there is scarcely in any Chess Opening one particular move or form of play universally accepted as *the* best, even amongst the magnates of the game, although there are some generally preferred, and therefore, so far, approaching finality in the favourite " Openings " of Chess.

Mr. J. H. Blackburne, in summing up the London Congress of 1883, in which he participated, said : " No striking novelties have been introduced by any of the players. The Ruy Lopez, as in all previous Tournaments, has been the most frequent *debut*. Zukertort, in his Openings, generally won on the Queen's side by adopting the English and the Queen's Gambit. Blackburne, Mason, Sellman, and Noa, have persistently adopted the French Defence. The Giuoco Piano has also more frequently been resorted to in this than in former Tournaments. No fewer than eighty-one games—or exactly one-half of the won games—were draws."

During Mr. Zukertort's recent visit to New Orleans, he expressed his lack of faith in the King's Knight's Gambit, and the King's Bishop's Gambit in particular. As a first move he condemns P-KB4 for either first or second player. He declared 3 P-KB4 a lost game for the defence in the Ruy Lopez, agreeing there with the " Synopsis," page 29. He approved of the Queen's Pawn Opening and the Evans attack.

The foregoing remarks show two things : First, that the Masters in supreme contests do not risk their reputation on Gambits ; second, that analysis of the Chess Openings is still in a transition stage. Such being the case, new ideas are welcome : and the eventual disposition of them is not always to be guessed. They will serve, in any event, to give variety to the game ; while the surprises

and neat little schemes of the Gambits will never bo disrelished. It often
happens to beginners in Chess that an autagonist makes a move or adopts a line
of play at an early stage that seems invincible. In such a case the "Synopsis"
will hardly fail to aid the student quickly, and often suggest a counter line to
turn the tables; for some of the bits of strategy most troublesome to learners
are wholly unsound. A good manual on the Openings is indispensable to the
player who would improve and keep step with the progress of Chess. Such a
text-book embodies the Chess wisdom of centuries, and productions of the mental
ingenuity of all nations, civilized and half civilized. Yet analysis of the Chess
Openings is not finished. There are, doubtless, errors to remove and important
discoveries to be made.

The Game of Chess is better known throughout the world now than any
other æsthetic human invention. It is the first thing, and the only thing thus
far to gain admittance into the poet's "parliament of man, the federation of the
world." It is the first language to spread around the globe, none the less
expressive for dispensing with words, and none the less intelligible for its
unerring appeal to reason and mental concentration, rather than to the diplomacy
of the tongue. The communion of two minds at Chess is not subject to the limits
of language or nationality. Some knowledge of so universal a pastime should be
regarded as a necessary accomplishment for all.

THE EVANS GAMBIT.

THIS beautiful Gambit is still in great favor. In tournament, as in off-hand play, the attack wins a majority of games. Analysis has not yet found an entirely satisfactory defence against the Evans. Dr Zukertort is of opinion that the Compromised is the best of the defences. For rapid, sparkling, intricate play, this Gambit is second to no other; and analysts are constantly called on to examine new lines of attack that may be adopted after a dozen moves have been played on each side. The variations in the following pages present some forcible ideas.

$1 \dfrac{\text{P-K4}}{\text{P-K4}}$ $2 \dfrac{\text{Kt-KB3}}{\text{Kt-QB3}}$ $3 \dfrac{\text{B-B4}}{\text{B-B4}}$ $4 \dfrac{\text{P-QKt4}}{\text{BxKtP}}$ 5 P-B3

Position after White's 5th move.

BLACK.

WHITE.

EVANS GAMBIT.

	1	2	3	4	5	6

(See Diagram on page 9.)

№	1	2	3	4	5	6
5	B-B4	B-R4				
6	Castles P-Q3	P-Q4 PxP				
7	P-Q4 PxP	Castles PxP (5)				
8	PxP B-Kt3	Q-Kt3 Q-B3				
9	Kt-B3 Kt-R4	P-K5 Q-Kt3				
10	B-KKt5 (1) P-KB3 (2)	KtxP KKt-K2				
11	B-B4 KtxB	B-R3 (6) R-QKtsq(7)		R-Qsq (11) Castles	P-Kt4	
12	Q-R4ch Q-Q2	Kt-Q5! (8) KtxKt!	P-Kt4	B-R3 P-QR3	KtxP R-QKtsq	
13	QxKt Q-B2	BxKt P-Kt4 (9)	KtxKt KtxKt	B-Q3 Q-K3	B-Q3 Q-K3	Q-Kt5 (14)
14	Kt-Q5! (3) P-Kt4	P-K6+	BxKt KxB	Kt-Q5 R-Ksq	Q-Kt2 P-QR3	
15	B-Kt3 B-K3		Q-R3ch K-Ksq!	Kt-Kt5 QxP	QKt-Q4(13)	
16	Q-R4ch B-Q2		QxB PxB	BxPch K-Bsq		
17	Q-R3 R-Bsq (4)		QxBP Q-Kt3 (10)	KtxKt+(12)		

(1) This move is disapproved on page 59 of the "Synopsis," but the "British Chess Magazine," May 1881 says: "There is now reason to believe that it is the most potent form of the attack." In the London Congress, 1883, Tschigorin made this move against Steinitz, and won on the 39th move.

(2) Best. If 10 Kt-K2, 11 Q-K2 is very cramping.

(3) Instead of 11 Q-Q3, as given in the "Synopsis," leading to a winning game for Black. The move in the text is the invention of Rosenthal. Black cannot reply Kt-K2, or B-Q2, without losing a Pawn, and his development becomes very difficult. The succeeding moves are from the Tschigorin-Steinitz game referred to, which will be found in the Book of the London Congress.

(4) Continued 18 KR-Ksq 18 P-Kt5, 19 KtxB 19 RPxKt, 20 Kt-Q2+

(5) The Compromised Defence.

(6) Now generally preferred to 11 Kt-K2. Dr Zukertort says it gives the most lasting form of attack in the "Compromised." The other plausible moves are 11 R-Ksq, and 11 R-Qsq, lately suggested by Mr W N Potter.

(7) Herr Anderssen was experimenting with this move at the time of his death. Mr Mortimer played it against both Steinitz and Zukertort at the London Congress, 1884.

(8) Recognised as a better continuation than the "Handbuch's" 12 Kt-QKt5.

(9) Mortimer played this move against Tschigorin in the London Congress; and 13 Kt-Qsq against Zukertort in the same meeting. He should have lost both games. Black's 11 R-QKtsq is unsatisfactory.

(10) Continued 18 Q-Q6 18 QxQ, 19 PxQ 19 B-R3, 20 KR-Ksqch, with a fine attack.

(11) Mr W N Potter's recent suggestion. The variations are from his analysis in "Land and Water."

(12) Mr Potter says (in "Land and Water") : "Mate next move, save for a useless check. If 15 Q-Kt5 or Q-R3, then 16 Kt-B6ch, and wins; or (in the latter case) 16 BxPch as before. After 14 Kt-Q5, there is 14 KtxKt, 15 BxPch, followed by 15 BxR, or 14 B-Kt5, 15 BxB 15 KtxB, 16 QxKt 16 KtxKt, 17 BxPch, followed by QxR, with a comfortable superiority in each case. We would, however, desire to point out that after 11 R-Qsq 11 Castles, White can at once play 12 B-Q3 12 Q-K3, 13 BxPch 13 K-Rsq, 14 Q-R4 14 P-KKt3, 15 Q-R3, or 15 B-Kt5, or 15 Kt-KKt5, with a warm attack in each case. There is also 14 B-Kt5, 15 B-Ktsq, or 15 B-Q3, or 15 B-QR3, with more or less satisfactory results. Altogether, we do not think that 11 Castles will be generally adopted."

(13) "If Black takes the Queen," remarks "Land and Water," "he loses the Gambit Pawn; and if he play Q-Q4, then 15 Kt-Kt3, and White seems to have at least as good a game as in the normal grooves of this Opening. As to 11 R-QKtsq, White answers 12 P-QR4, and smiles. There remains now but 11 B-Kt3, 12 Q-R3 (among other replies) 12 Castles, 13 Kt-K2, or 13 B-KB4, or 13 B-Q3, with a sense of comfort. Altogether we think we have made good our case, which is, that 11 R-Qsq ought to be reckoned as a candidate for adoption. We purpose dealing with P-Q Kt4, and our ideas will crop out in the form of additional variations. To proceed: 11 R-Qsq 11 P-QKt4, 12 KtxP 12 R-QKtsq, 13 B-Q3 13 Q-K3, 14 Q-R4 14 P-QR3, 15 QxB 15 RxKt, or PxKt (if KtxQ, then KtxPch, with an undoubted advantage), 16 QxBP, and White has rather the better game. Instead of 14 P-QR3 Black may play 14 B-R3. White has three replies, viz.: 15 QxB, 15 KtxPch, and 15 QKt-Q4. The two last named continuations branch out into a luxurious display of variations and sub-variations, some of them highly interesting. As net result, White, adopting any one of these three replies, can at least stand his ground."

(14) "This may seem formidable, but as a matter of fact, there are two replies—one being 14 P-KR3 14 Q-QKt5, 15 QxQ 15 BxQ, 16 KtxPch 16 K-Qsq (16 K-Bsq, 17 B-KB4), 17 Kt-QKt5 17 P-QR3, 18 Kt-Q6 18 B-B6, 19 R-Ktsq, or KtxPch, and White for choice. Instead of 15 BxQ, Black may play 15 KtxQ, wherefore 16 KtxRP 16 KtxB, 17 RxKt, and, while claiming no superiority for White, we must express doubt whether his bold bid for a numerical superiority can be proved to be a disastrous stroke for him. However, there is the other answer, viz.: 14 B-K2 (instead of P-KR3). If Black reply with P-QR3, then 15 Kt-Kt5 15 Q-B4 best, 16 P-Kt4, with a promising attack. If Black answer 14 B-K2 with 14 Q-QKt5, then 15 QxQ 15 KtxQ (15 BxQ, 16 KtxPch), 16 B-Q2, with a good game. Altogether there seems to be plenty of scope for the analyst in 11 R-Qsq, answered by P-QKt4. Our method (continues Mr Potter) of improving the attack is impugned by " W W," than whom there is no more eminent authority amongst English analysts. He writes as follows: 'If your move of 11 KR-Qsq is met by 11 Castles, and White then plays 12 B-R3, Black's reply should be 12 P-QKt4, not P-QR3, which loses too much time; and if 12 B-Q3, not 12 Q-K3 (which is all right before Castling), but 12 Q-R4, and I cannot see that the attack is at all strengthened.' We mentioned two continuations for White, namely, 12 B-R3, and 12 B-Q3. These are the continuations which " W W " takes up; he replying to the former with P-QKt4, and to the latter with Q-R4. After premising that these moves are of such importance that they ought to be considered, though we found it necessary to limit ourselves previously to more patent defences, we will proceed to express our ideas analytically; 11 R-Qsq 11 Castles, 12 B-R3 12 P-QKt4, 13 B-Q3 13 Q-R4, 14 Kt-K4 14 P-Kt5, 15 Kt-Kt3 15 Q-Kt5, 16 B-Kt2, with a game such as any expert would be well satisfied with. White might also have proceeded with 16 P-KR3 16 Q-K3, 17 B-B4 17 Q-Kt3, 18 B-QBsq, with a satisfactory game, nor will it have been lost sight of that he could, if so choosing, have forced a draw in this variation. As 14 P-Kt5 evidently conforms to White's desires, we must see if Black can do anything better. 14 B-Kt2 would be sufficiently met by 15 BxKt 15 KtxB, 16 QxKtP, with a good game. 14 B-Kt3 admits of 15 BxKtP 15 R-Ktsq, 16 Q-Q3 16 R- Kt5, 17 QBxKt 17 KtxB best, 18 BxP 18 R-Qsq, 19 B-KKt4 19 RxQ best, 20 BxQ, and White has regained both the Gambit Pawns. The prettiness of this variation, arising as it does from 16 R-Ksq, which is Black's most plausible move, is sufficient justification for giving it, but the very defensive move of 16 R-Qsq was better. However, as against that line, White would be content with having regained one of the Gambit Pawns, without having suffered in position. If brilliancy be White's object, he may answer 16 R-Qsq, with 17 Kt-B6ch 17 PxKt, 18 PxP 18 BxPch, (if Kt-K3 then BxKt), 19 KxB 19 QxB, 20 QxQ 20 R xQ, 21 PxKt 21 R-Ksq, 22 QR-Bsq, but we do not mean to say that we recommend this course, Still, the fact that White has so many resources open to his selection, would of itself cause 14 B-Kt3 to be shirked, even were that move in itself good. There is, however, 14 R-Ktsq, but that is so slow a method of proceeding, that we would simply answer it with 15 P-KR3. However, lest we may have gone beyond the reader's range, let us retrace our steps; 11 R-Qsq 11 Castles, 12 B-R3 12 P-QKt4, 13 B-Q3 13 Q-R4, 14 Kt-K4 (a) 14 R-Ktsq, 15 P-KR3, and we should look upon the game as undoubtedly in White's favor, for now he threatens Kt(K4)-Kt5, with direful effects. Should the Knight get there, Black cannot play P-KR3, as hitherto, on account of P-KR4, nor can he play P-KR3 beforehand, to prevent its getting there, for then comes another destructive move, viz.: Kt-Kt3. It is clear, therefore, 15 P-KR3 must be attended to. Some may suggest, as a reply, 15 P-Kt5, 16 B-Kt2 16 Kt-Kt3, but then 17 Kt-Kt3 17 Q-R3, 18 B-QBsq 18 Kt-Q5, 19 Kt-B5, winning a Piece, and good enough, though we imagine that White could also have profitably played 17 Kt(K4)-Kt5. Here we must leave the variations arising from 12 B-R3 12 P-QKt4, while, as to 12 B-Q3 12 Q-R4, we will content ourselves for the present with proposing 13 B-R3 13 P-QKt4, 14 Kt-K4, which is the same line of play, arising by transposition."

(a) An article in "The British Chess Magazine," for May 1884, calls this move a real novelty, and adds: "Clearly, in Mr Potter's own words, 11 R-Qsq for White, in the Compromised Defence, is a candidate for adoption.

EVANS GAMBIT.

(See Diagram on page 9.)

5	6	7	8	9
B-B4 ——	P-Q4 / PxP	Castles / P-Q3	PxP / B-Kt3	P-Q5 / Kt-R4
10 B-Kt2 / Kt-K2	**11** B-Q3 / Castles	**12** Kt-B3 / Kt-Kt3	**13** Kt-K2 / P-QB4	**14** Q-Q2 / P-B3
15 QR-Bsq / R-Ktsq	**16** Kt-Kt3 / B-B2	**17** Kt-B5 / P-Kt4	**18** K-Rsq / P-B5	**19** B-K2 / P-QKt5 (1)
20 BxQBP (2) / KtxB	**21** RxKt / B-R3	**22** RxB / QxR (3)	**23** R-Bsq / Q-Q2!	**24** Kt(B3)-Q4

	7	8	9	10	11	12
24	Kt-K2	Kt-K4			KR-Bsq	
	KtxKtP!	Kt(Q1)-K6			Kt-K6	
25	Q-Kt5 (4)	Kt-B5	R-B2		Kt-K4	RxRch
	Kt(Kt7)B5	RxKt	P-KR3 (6)		Kt(K6)xP	QxR
26	KtxKt	BxR	Kt-B5	Q-R5	Kt-B5	Q-Kt4
	KtxKt	QKtxKtP	Q-Q4	BxKt	Kt-K6	QKtxKtP
27	QxKP (5)	R-B2	KtxB	QPxB	QxKt	Q-B8ch
		Kt-KB5	R-B7	Kt(B5)xP	Kt-R6ch	QxQ
28		BxRP	Q-R5	RxKt	K-Bsq!	BxQ
		Q-Kt5ch+	RxR	KtxR	Q-B4+	Kt-KB5
29			KxR	KxKt		K-B2!
			QxRPch	R-B7ch		KtxPch+
30			R-Kt2	K-Kt3		
			KtxQPch+	Q-K3		
31				Q-Q8ch		
32				K-R2		
				Q-R4		
33				QxP+		

(1) This page is devoted to a game between Louisville (White) and Chicago (Black). An analysis of it, by the late Hon. Bland Ballard, of Kentucky, was published in "The Louisville Monthly Magazine," from which these notes are condensed.

(2) The books proceed 20 B-Q4 20 P-B6, 21 Q-Qsq 21 B-Kt3, 22 P-QR3, and call the game even.

(3) If BxR White mates in four moves.

(4) If 25 KxKt, 26 R-B7 26 QxR, 27 Kt-K6ch+. If 26 Q-Kt5, 27 RxKtch+

(5) Immediately fatal; but Black's game is lost. If 27 K-Rsq, 28 P-B3 28 Q-Kt3!, 29 KtxP 29 R-Ktsq, 30 P-Kt4+. If 27 Q-R4, 28 P-Kt4 28 Q-R6, 29 Q-B4 29 QR-Bsq, 30 Kt-R6ch+.

(6) White cannot play 26 R-B7, because Black would reply Q-Kt4, threatening mate. Judge Ballard is, therefore, of the opinion that White, on his 18th move, should play P-KR3, instead of the book move, K-Rsq.

EVANS GAMBIT.

	13	14	15	16

(See Diagram on page 9.)

	13	14	15	16
5	B-K2 (1)			B-Bsq (7)
6	Q-Kt3	P-Q4		P-Q4
	Kt-R3	Kt-R4 (4)		Q-K2
7	P-Q4	KtxP (5)	Q-Q3	Castles
	Kt-R4	KtxB	KtxB	P-Q3
8	Q-R4	KtxKt	QxKt	Q-Kt3
	KtxB	P-Q4	Kt-B3	P-KKt3
9	QxKt	PxP	KtxP	PxP
	Kt-Kt5 (2)	QxP	Castles	PxP
10	P-KR3 (3)	Kt-K3—	P-Q5	R-Qsq
	Kt-B3	Q-Qsq—	KtxKP	B-R3
11	PxP —		QxKt	QKt-Q2
	P-Q4—		B-B3	Q-B3
12			Castles	B-R3+
			R-Ksq (6)	

(1) **This** move is pronounced bad on page 52 (Cols. 1 and 2) of the "Synopsis." The variations here presented are from the "Schachzeitung," 1879.

(2) This move is not given in the "Synopsis."

(3) White could probably do better by waiting and developing.

(4) PxP is the move in Cook.

(5) If 7 B-Q3 7 PxP, or 7 B-QKt3 7 Kt-KB3.

(6) Game played by correspondence. Continued . 13 P-KB4 13 P-Q3, 14 R-B3 14 PxKt, 15 P-B5 15 P-KKt3, 16 PxP 16 BPxP, 17 B-R3 17 B-B4, 18 RxB 18 PxR, 19 QxBP 19 B-Kt2, 20 Q-K4 20 Q-B3, 21 Kt-Q2 21 Q-B5, 22 R-Qsq 22 B-Bsq, 23 B-Bsq 23 B-B4ch, 24 K-Rsq 24 R-KBsq, 25 QxQ 25 RxQ, 26 Kt-B3 26 R-B4, 27 P-KR3 27 P-K5, 28 Kt-Kt5 28 QR-KBsq+.

(7) Played by Mr Steinitz against Tschigorin, in the Vienna Congress, 1882. Mr Tschigorin (White) won on the 40th move.

THE KNIGHT'S GAME OF RUY LOPEZ.

THIS powerful attack is adopted oftener than any other in the open games in match and tournament play. It is also a favorite in correspondence games, Paris playing it, the present year (1884), against Vienna, and Edinburgh against Glasgow. It is one of the most common Openings witnessed in Clubs and off-hand play. In a recent article, in "The British Chess Magazine," Mr Freeborough says:

"The difference of opinion that exists with regard to the defence to the Lopez, shows that the true theory has yet to be discovered. It is still undetermined whether it is better to play 3 P-QR3, or let the first player's Bishop stand on QKt5. The latter has been held of late to be the only 'absolutely correct defence.' The 'Synopsis' alludes to 3 P-QR3, as a loss of time in certain variations. Mr Steinitz has repeatedly pointed out its disadvantages. In the early part of the London Tournament (1883) Zukertort played 3 Kt-B3, but later he played 3 P-QR3, his opponents being Steinitz, Winawer, Rosenthal, and Mackenzie. As an annotator he is silent on the subject."

The Ruy Lopez was adopted fifty-three times in the London Congress, which was more than one-fourth the number of games played. The second players adopted for their third move, P-QR3 twenty-seven times, Kt-KB3 nineteen times, P-KKt3 four times, and Kt-Q5 three times. Nine of the players—out of fourteen —adopted 3 P-QR3, and five chose 3 Kt-KB3; but, while all the players who at times played the latter move, at times also chose the former, four out of the nine never played 3 Kt-KB3. Messrs Englisch and Mackenzie always moved 3 P-QR3; Dr Zukertort having about equally favored both moves; and M Rosenthal—though also using both—giving the preference to 3 Kt-KB3; while Mr Steinitz never played the last mentioned move.

After 3 P-QR3, chosen twenty-seven times by Black, White replied in twenty-five cases with 4 B-R4, to which Black answered in twenty-two cases with 4 Kt-B3, twice with 4 KKt-K2 (Steinitz), and once with 4 P-KKt3 (Steinitz). These facts make it evident that the best third move for Black in this Opening is still undetermined, though 3 P-QR3 and 3 Kt-B3 are most frequently adopted.

RUY LOPEZ KNIGHT'S GAME.

$$1 \ \frac{\text{P-K4}}{\text{P-K4}} \quad 2 \ \frac{\text{Kt-KB3}}{\text{Kt-QB3}} \quad 3 \ \frac{\text{B-Kt5}}{\text{P-KKt3 (1)}}$$

	1	2	3	4	5	6
4	BxKt / QPxB	KtPxB	Castles / B-Kt2	P-Q4 / KtxP	PxP	P-B3 (5) / B-Kt2
5	KtxP / Q-Q5	KtxP / Q-K2	P-B3 (2) / QKt-K2	KtxKt / PxKt	BxKt / QPxB	P-Q4 / PxP
6	Kt-KB3 / QxPch	P-Q4 / P-Q3	P-Q4 / PxP	QxP / Q-B3	QxP / QxQ	PxP (6) / QKt-K2
7	Q-K2 / QxQch	KtxQBP / QxPch	PxP / P-QB3	B-K3 / B-Kt2	KtxQ / B-Q2	B-Kt5 / P-QB3
8	KxQ / B-KKt5	Q-K2 / QxQch	B-R4 / Kt-B3	P-QB3 / QxQ	Castles / B-Kt2	B-QR4 / Kt-B3
9	P-KR3 / BxKtch	KxQ / B-QKt2	P-K5 / Kt-Q4	PxQ / P-QR3	P-QB3 / Castles	P-K5 (7) / Kt-K5
10	KxB / Castles+ or B-Kt2+	P-Q5 / BxKt+ or K-Q2+	Kt-B3 / Kt-Kt3	B-R4 (3) / P-QB4	B-Kt5 / P-B3	B-R4 / Q-R4ch
11			B-Kt3— / P-Q4 —	P-K5 / P-QKt4	B-K3 / P-QB4	QKt-Q2 / Kt-B4
12				B-B2 / B-Kt2	Kt-Kt3 / P-Kt3	B-KKt3 / KtxKt
13				Castles / Kt-K2+	QKt-Q2 / Kt-R3 (4)	KtxKt / KtxP+

(1) This defence is allotted but one column in the "Synopsis." See page 29, Column 30. The result is given as unfavorable for Black. But we notice that the defence has been adopted by Glasgow in one of its pending Correspondence games with Edinburgh. The analysis of the defence on this page, except Col. 6, is by Mr A P Barnes, of New York, and was originally published four years ago in "The Canadian (Montreal) Spectator." The defence merits more attention than it has received. Mr Barnes says that it can be relied on for rather the better game; but this is probably claiming too much.

(2) If 5 Kt-B3 5 Kt-Q5, 6 KtxKt 6 PxKt, 7 Kt-K2 7 P-QB3, 8 B-R4 8 Kt-K2+. If 5 P-Q4 5 KtxP, 6 KtxKt 6 PxKt, 7 P-K5 7 P-QB3, 8 B-R4 8 P-Q3+.

(3) 10 B-B4 10 Kt-B3.

(4) Edinburgh-Glasgow Correspondence game, which was concluded 19th June 1884, by a victory for Black. The remaining moves are 14 BxKt 14 BxB, 15 KR-Ksq 15 KR-Ksq, 16 P-B3 16 P-R4, 17 Kt-KBsq 17 P-R5, 18 Kt(Kt3)-Q2 18 B-K3, 19 R-K2 19 R-Q6, 20 Kt-Ktsq 20 R-Q8, 21 K-B2 21 KR-Qsq, 22 P-QKt3 22 R-B8, 23 R-Ksq 23 R-Q8, 24 RxR 24 RxR, 25 P-Kt3 25 B-R6, and White resigned.

(5) If 4 Kt-B3 4 Kt-Q5, 5 KtxKt 5 PxKt, 6 Kt-K2 6 P-QB3, 7 B-R4 7 B-Kt2+.

(6) 6 BxKt 6 QPxB, 7 PxP 7 B-Kt5, 8 P-K5 8 BxKt+. If Black 6 PxP, 7 BxQPch 7 QxB 8 Qx Qch 8 BxQ, 9 KtxP 9 BxKtch 10 PxB 10 Castles+.

(7) If 9 BxKt 9 BxB, 10 P-K5 10 B-Kt2, 11 Castles 11 Castles, 12 Kt-Ksq 12 Kt-B4, 13 Kt-B2 13 P-Q3, 14 P-B4 14 PxP, 15 BPxP 15 Q-Kt3, 16 B-Kt3 16 KtxP, 17 KtxKt 17 BxP+.

RUY LOPEZ KNIGHT'S GAME.

$$1 \ \frac{\text{P-K4}}{\text{P-K4}} \qquad 2 \ \frac{\text{Kt-KB3}}{\text{Kt-QB3}} \qquad 3 \ \frac{\text{B-Kt5}}{\text{Kt-B3}}$$

	7	8	9	10	11	12
	Vienna 1882 Congress.	London 1883 Congress.	Match 1883 Paris.	Match 1884 Baltimore.	London 1883 Congress.	London 1883 Congress.
	Zukertort Englisch	Tschigorin Zukertort	De Rivière Tschigorin	Sellman Zukertort	Englisch Zukertort	Steinitz Rosenthal
4	Castles KtxP				P-Q3 P-Q3	B-B4
5	P-Q4 B-K2		P-QR3		Kt-B3 P-KKt3	P-B3 Q-K2
6	Q-K2 Kt-Q3	P-Q5 Kt-Q3	BxKt (5) QPxB		P-KR3 B-Kt2	Castles Castles
7	BxKt KtPxB	BxKt QPxB	Q-K2 P-KB4	R-Ksq B-KB4	B-K3 B-Q2	P-Q4 B-Kt3
8	PxP Kt-Kt2	PxP (4) P-B3	PxP B-B4	Kt-B3 ? KtxKt	Q-Q2 P-KR3	BxKt KtPxB
9	Kt-B3 (1) Kt-B4	PxP BxP	QKt-Q2 KtxKt	RxPch B-K3	Castles Kt-KKtsq	KtxP P-Q3 (7)
10	Kt-Q4 Castles	B-K3 Castles	BxKt Castles	PxKt B-Q3	P-Q4 PxP	KtxP QxP
11	R-Qsq (2) Q-Ksq	QKt-Q2 Kt-B2	QR-Qsq Q-K2	R-Ksq Castles (6)	KtxP KKt-K2	Kt-Kt4 P-B4
12	Kt-B5 P-B3	Q-K2 P-KB4	B-K2 B-K3	B-Kt5 Q-Bsq	QR-Qsq Kt-K4	Kt-B2 B-R3
13	B-R6 Kt-K3 (3)	Kt-Kt3 P-B5	P-B4 P-R3	Q-Q2 P-B3	B-K2 P-KKt4	R-Ksq Q-R5
14	Q-Kt4 R-B2	B-B5 P-K5	P-KR4 QR-Qsq	B-B4 Q-Q2	P-B4 PxP	P-B3 P-Q4
15	B-K3 K-Rsq	KKt-Q4 P-B6	R-Bsq R-Q2	BxB PxB	BxP KKt-Kt3	R-K5 PxP
16	KtxB QxKt	Q-Kt5 Q-Bsq	P-KKt3 KR-Qsq	P-QR3 B-Kt5	B-K3 Kt-R5	PxP Kt-Q2
17	PxP QxP	KR-Qsq B-R3	P-Kt3 P-QKt4	Q-B4 BxKt	R-B2 R-KKtsq	P-KKt3 Q-R6
18	Q-QR4 Q-Kt3	Q-R4 Kt-Kt4	P-R5 PxP	QxB KR-Ksq	K-Rsq P-QB3	R-Ksq QR-Ksq
19	R-Q2 P-B4	KtxP PxKt	PxP Q-B2	Q-Q3 R-K3	Kt-Kt3 B-KBsq	B-K3 R-K3
20	Q-Kt3 P-Q3+	R-Q7 PxP+	Kt-Q2 B-Kt5+	P-B3 QR-Ksq+	BxKRP KtxP+	Kt-B3 Kt-B3+ (8)

For Notes see page 19.

RUY LOPEZ KNIGHT'S GAME.

$$1\ \frac{\text{P-K4}}{\text{P-K4}} \qquad 2\ \frac{\text{Kt-KB3}}{\text{Kt-QB3}} \qquad 3\ \frac{\text{B-Kt5}}{\text{P-QR3}}\ (9)$$

	13	14	15	16	17	18
	Nash Cor. Tourney No 3	Match 1882 Philadelphia.	New Orleans 1883.	New Orleans 1883.	Vienna 1882 Congress.	Match 1882 Philadelphia.
	Blake Vincent	**Martinez** Steinitz	McConnell Steinitz	McConnell Steinitz	Blackburne Steinitz	**Martinez** Steinitz
4	B-R4 / Kt-B3	KKt-K2				
5	Castles / KtxP	P-Q4 / PxP				
6	R-Ksq (10) / Kt-B4	KtxP / KtxKt				P-B3 (13) / PxP
7	BxKt / QPxB	QxKt / Kt-B3				KtxP / Kt-Kt3
8	P-Q4 / Kt-K3	BxKt / QPxB	Q-K3 / B-K2	P-QKt4 / P-Q3		Castles / B-K2
9	KtxP / B-K2	QxQch / KxQ	Castles / Castles	Q-K3 / B-K3	P-QB3 / P-QB4	Kt-Q5 / Castles
10	B-K3 / Castles	B-K3 / B-K3	Kt-B3 / Q-Ksq	Castles / P-QB3	Q-Qsq / B-Kt2	KtxBch / QxKt
11	Kt-QB3 / P-B3	P-KB4 (12) / P-B3	Kt-Q5 / B-Qsq	P-KB4 / Q-Q2	Castles / Q-Q2	B-B2 / P-Q3
12	Kt-B3 / R-Ksq (11)	K-B2 / B-Q3	B-Kt3 / P-Q3	P-B5 / BxB	R-Ksq / P-B5	B-Kt5 / P-B3
13	Kt-K2 / Kt-Bsq	Kt-Q2 / K-Q2	P-KB4 / K-Rsq	RPxB / Q-R2	B-B2 / Kt-Kt3	B-Q2 / K-Rsq
14	Q-Q3 / B-KKt5	Kt-B3 / QR-Ksq	P-B5 / Kt-K4	Kt-B3 / QxQ	Kt-Q2 / B-K2	P-KR3 / KKt-K4
15	Kt-Q2 / Q-Q2	P-K5 / PxP	P-B6 / R-KKtsq	BxQ / P-B3	Kt-Bsq / Castles	B-B3 / KtxKtch
16	Kt-KKt3 / Kt-Kt3	PxP / B-K2	Kt-K7 / BxKt	R-R5 / K-Q2	Q-R5 / QR-Ksq	QxKt / Kt-K4
17	P-KR3 / B-K3	QR-Qsqch / K-Bsq	PxB / QxP	KR-QRsq / Kt-Bsq	Kt-Kt3 / B-Qsq	Q-Kt3 / B-K3
18	P-KB4 / Kt-R5	P-QKt3 / KR-Bsq+	B-Q2 / B-K3	RxRP / RxR	Kt-B5 / P-B3	P-B4 / Kt-Q2
19	Kt(Q2)-K4 / K-Rsq		B-B3 / BxB	RxR / B-K2	P-QR4 / P-Q4	Q-R4 / B-Ktsq
20	R-K2 / BxKRP+		RPxB+	Kt-R2 / P-B4 Drawn.	PxKtP+	QR-Ksq— / QR-Ksq—

For Notes see page 19.

C

RUY LOPEZ KNIGHT'S GAME.

$$1\ \frac{\text{P-K4}}{\text{P-K4}}\qquad 2\ \frac{\text{Kt-KB3}}{\text{Kt-QB3}}\qquad 3\ \frac{\text{B-Kt5}}{}$$

	19	20	21	22	23	24
	Vienna 1882 Congress.	Vienna 1882 Congress.	London 1883 Congress.	Corresponde. Match 1884.	New York 1883.	Match, New Orleans.
	Fleissig Mackenzie	Weiss Mackenzie	Steinitz Zukertort	Paris Vienna	Teed Steinitz	Wurm Blackmar
3	P-QR3					P-B4 (20)
4	B-R4 / Kt-B3				BxKt / QPxB	P-Q3 (21) / PxP (22)
5	Castles / KtxP	Kt-B3 / B-B4	P-Q3 / P-Q3		Kt-B3 / P-B3	PxP / Q-B3
6	P-Q4 / P-QKt4	KtxP / KtxKt	P-B3 / P-KKt3	B-K2	Kt-K2 / P-QB4	Castles / B-Q3
7	B-Kt3 / P-Q4	P-Q4 / B-Q3	P-Q4 / P-QKt4	QKt-Q2 / Castles	Kt-Kt3 / P-KKt3	Kt-B3 / KKt-K2
8	PxP / B-K3	P-B4 / Kt-B3 (15)	B-B2 / B-QKt2	Kt-Bsq / Kt-Q2	P-Q3 / Kt-K2	Kt-Q5 / KtxKt
9	P-B3 (14) / B-QB4	P-K5 / B-Kt5	P-Q5 / Kt-K2	B-K3 / P-B4	B-K3 / Kt-B3	QxKt / Kt-K2
10	QKt-Q2 / Castles	PxKt / QxP	P-QR4 / PxP (17)	PxP / RxP	P-B3 / B-K3	Q-Kt3 / P-KR3
11	B-B2 / P-B4	B-K3 / Castles	BxPch / Kt-Q2	B-Kt3ch / K-Rsq	Q-B2 / Q-Q2	B-K2 / P-QKt3
12	Kt-Kt3 / B-Kt3	Castles / BxKt	P-R4 / P-R3	P-KR4 / Q-Ksq	P-Kt3 / P-KR4	Kt-Q2 / B-Kt2
13	QKt-Q4 / KtxKt	PxB / Kt-K2	P-R5 / P-Kt4	Kt-Kt5 / Kt-B4	P-KR3 / P-QKt4	P-KB3 / Kt-Kt3
14	KtxKt / Q-K2	P-B4 / P-Q4	P-KKt4 / Kt-Bsq	B-Q5 / R-Bsq	Castles / P-Kt4	Kt-B4 / B-B4ch
15	B-Kt3 / BxKt	PxP / KtxP	B-K3 / B-K2	QBxKt / PxB	K-R2 / P-R5	K-Rsq / Kt-B5
16	PxB / P-B5	Q-Q2 / B-B4	QKt-Q2 / Castles	Kt-Kt3 / B-Q2	Kt-K2 / B-Q3	BxKt / QxB
17	P-B3 / Kt-Kt6!	B-B2 / Q-KKt3	B-B2 / P-QB3 (18)	Q-K2 / R-B5	KKt-Ktsq / Kt-K2	QR-Qsq / P-KR4
18	PxKt / PxP	B-KKt3 / Kt-B3	P-B4 / Kt(B1-Kt3)	B-K6 / R-Qsq	P-B3 / K-B2	Kt-R5 / B-QBsq
19	R-Ksq / Q-R5	QR-Ksq / Kt-K5	Kt-KKtsq / Q-B2	Kt(Kt3-K4) / BxKt	K-Rsq / KR-Qsq	Q-Q5 / R-QKtsq
20	B-K3 / Q-R7ch+	Q-K3 / P-Kt4+ (16)	P-Kt3 / KR-Bsq	BxB / QxB (19)	P-Q4+	Kt-B6+

For Notes see page 19.

NOTES, to pages 16, 17, and 18.

(1) B-K3 or Kt-Q4 is the usual play.

(2) Threatening KtxP.

(3) Capturing the B would lose.

(4) Mr Ranken prefers KtxP, as giving a perfectly even game. The text move gives Black an immediate advantage of position.

(5) Pronounced best by M Rosenthal.

(6) Mr Sellman says the weakness of White's eighth move now becomes apparent. Black has effectually parried the attack, and comes out of the mêlée with the advantage of two Bishops against Knight and Bishop.

(7) Dr Zukertort thinks this sacrifice of a P would prove unsound against the best defence.

(8) This page gives the preference to games won by the defence; the main difficulty with the Ruy Lopez being to meet the many resources of the vigorous attack.

(9) In notes to this move, Mr J Russell says, authorities are divided as to the respective merits of 3 P-QR3 and 3 Kt-B3. An examination of many games favors the conclusion that 3 P-QR3 gives more freedom to the defending player. It is difficult to perceive how this move can properly be described as "lost time," unless White choose to capture the Kt at once, as recommended by Anderssen; and by a rapid exchange of Pieces, endeavour to bring about an advantageous end game. But Black has two Bishops and an open Queen's file, which should more than compensate for his doubled Pawns. It may be safely affirmed that 3 P-QR3 is in no case objectionable; and in many variations is to Black's advantage.

(10) P-Q4 is a more lasting attack.

(11) The moves so far are identical with those in a game between Mrs Gilbert and Mr Gossip, won by the former. Mr Gossip (Black) played 12 P-KB4.

(12) This weakens the KP. The proper move was P-KB3.

(13) A venturesome sacrifice. It led in this case to a finely contested game of 81 moves, and a draw.

(14) B-K3 is the usual move.

(15) Mr Sellman says the move usually recommended is Kt-Kt3, but the move in the text seems preferable, as it embarrasses White's development after 10 QxP.

(16) Clearing the position at Ksq for his Rooks.

(17) Leaving the beaten track.

(18) Black took the attack at this point, and won after a hard contest of ninety moves.

(19) Continued 21 PxB 21 QxP, 22 QxQ 22 RxQ, 23 K-K2 23 R-Q4, 24 P-KB3 24 K-Ktsq, and the game is still in progress.

(20) Mr C A Maurian says this Counter Gambit yields the second player a very inferior game, in the opinion of most authorities, but against an opponent not well versed in the books, it is apt to produce a strong counter attack.

(21) 4 P-Q4 or Q-K2 are also good.

(22) 4 Kt-Q5 is preferable.

THE FRENCH DEFENCE.

THIS conservative, though not necessarily slow method of replying to the attack's 1 P-K4, is very much in vogue in formal and off-hand play. It was played forty-nine times at the London Congress of 1883. Blackburne, Mason, Noa, Sellman, and Winawer defended with the French, forty-three times in the total of forty-nine games. Tschigorin chose it twice, Skipworth three times, and Mackenzie once. The remaining six of the fourteen contestants, Bird, Englisch, Mortimer, Rosenthal, Steinitz, and Zukertort, did not play it at all.

In the forty-nine games the attack proceeded 2 P-Q4 forty-six times, 2 P-K5 twice (Steinitz), and 2 P-KB4 once (Englisch).

The old line of play, laid down in Staunton's "Handbook," viz. : 1 P-K4 1 P-K3, 2 P-Q4 2 P-Q4, 3 PxP 3 PxP, was adopted at the Congress but eleven times. A more recent form, not spoken of in the "Handbook," viz. : 1 P-K4 1 P-K3, 2 P-Q4 2 P-Q4, 3 Kt-QB3, was adopted by the attack thirty-three times. The defence replied 3 Kt-KB3 thirty-one times, and B-QKt5 twice. This more modern attack, 3 Kt-QB3, was invariably chosen by Bird, Blackburne, Mackenzie, Mortimer, Noa, Tschigorin, and Winawer. Mr Sellman always adhered to the older 3 PxP, the remaining contestants varying the move.

After 3 Kt-QB3 3 Kt-KB3 White adopted 4 B-KKt5 eighteen times, and 4 PxP nine times, a majority of 2 to 1 in favor of the former. Blackburne and Mortimer adopted both forms. Invariably Steinitz, Mackenzie, Winawer, Mason, Bird, and Englisch attacked with 4 B-KKt5, and Noa, Tschigorin, and Rosenthal with 4 PxP.

Mr Thomas Long remarks of the frequent employment of the French Defence in the London Congress that :

"We might, at first sight, naturally conclude from these figures, that one considerable section of these fine players hold the theory that, in the battle for position in the 'Openings' of Chess, Black cannot hope to equalise the game in as short a period (if at all) by adopting the open game of 1 P-K4, as when he moves 1 P-K3, but we must consider that it by no means follows that, because the second player adopts the 'French,' the 'Sicilian,' or 'Irregular' game, that he is of opinion that the attack, in theory, must obtain the better position in the open game. He may be desirous of avoiding some particular Opening, with some especial antagonist.

"Likewise with the first player ; it does not necessarily follow that, because he sometimes opens with some irregular or bizarre move, as 1 Kt-KB3 or 1 Kt-QB3, as in the Congress games, that he holds that the defence must obtain the better position in the open regular, of 1 P-K4. He too, doubtless, has his object at the time he thus commences his game—for we find the same players moving P-K4, or otherwise, on the first move.

"The fact is, theory holds—however practice may vary—that the second player can equalise the game in every Opening commencing with 1 P-K4 on both sides—in some Openings a little earlier than in others—and also that the first player need have no fear (where, as in the Gambits, he does not make sacrifice of material) of even the best defences in any of the open games."

In the autumn of 1883 "Land and Water" published the following appreciative estimate of this Opening :

"It is now nearly forty years since Staunton commended the French Defence, inasmuch as it 'by nullifying the advantage of the first move, gives a higher tone and character to the game than it possesses while chance is an admitted element of the struggle.' The accuracy of this opinion has been, to a large extent, verified by the Opening's subsequent career; for though the adoption of 1 P-K3 by Black, does not entirely deprive White of the profit derived from playing first, yet at any rate it goes nearer than any other defence, to placing the players on an equality at starting. Nevertheless, though this has at no time been doubted, the French Defence was, until a comparatively recent period, treated with much scorn. It was considered a mean and cowardly method of opening. Now all is changed, and its adoption by experts of the first rank, is frequent in important games. Mr Blackburne, as is well known, scarcely ever plays otherwise. It was a favorite with the late Mr De Vere, and also with Mr W N Potter, in his day of active play, and it is likewise much used by Mr Mason; so that altogether it might much more appropriately be called the Anglo-Saxon Defence, than the name which its adoption by Labourdonnais against McDonnell caused it to receive. It scarcely needs mentioning that Labourdonnais was not the first, by a good many, to move 1 P-K3 as second player. How old the Opening is no one knows; but, as Lucena alludes thereto, it is very clear that Chess players four centuries ago opened their games in this fashion. The special features of the French Defence (in its normal grooves) are very easily stated. The Bishops on both sides become immediately liberated, and capable of a free action. No clogging, no blocking up. The King's Knight comes quietly out, and Castling may quickly take place. As neither side can hinder that operation, so, and for that very reason, a speedy resource to Castling by each player becomes advisable, lest the adversary's King's Rook, which so early takes part in the fray, should prove mischevious. The Queens' Knights are also fit for fighting, and the Queens' Rooks are in nowise prevented from responding to any call for their services. The rapid development of Pieces on both sides is, therefore, a special feature of the French Defence. As a consequence thereof, it must be admitted that there is in the Opening, a want of that richness which attends a slow, complex development, and also a deficiency of sparkling positions. Another notable feature is the marked augmentation of the power of the Bishops, with its corollary in a sensible diminution of scope on the part of the Knights, so that the latter are sometimes only useful as corks, for the stopping up of diagonals. A third very remarkable peculiarity of this Opening is the active part played by the Rooks therein, while as a winding-up characteristic it is worth noticing that the Queen often has to play the undignified part of staying behind Bishops, and backing them up. All these points represent one and the same meaning. There is a free board, and this is the ear-mark of the French Defence."

THE following is the position after White's 10th move, in the game between Messrs Weiss and Schwarz, given in column 7, page 23.

BLACK.

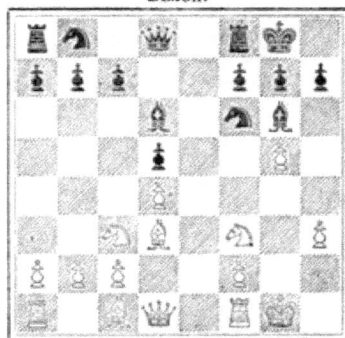

WHITE.

FRENCH DEFENCE.

	1	2	3	4	5	6
	Vienna 1882 Congress.	Vienna 1882 Congress.	Vienna 1882 Congress.	Match 1883 Havana.	Match 1882 Philadalphia.	Vienna 1882 Congress.
	Steinitz Schwarz	Steinitz Mason	Steinitz Fleissig	Steinitz Golmayo	Steinitz Martinez	Steinitz Winawer
1	P-K4 / P-K3					
2	P-K5 (1) / P-QB4 (2)		P-Q4		P-QR3 (5)	P-KB3! (7)
3	P-KB4 / Kt-QB3 (3)		PxP en pass / BxP	PxP	P-KB4 / P-Q4	P-Q4 / P-QB4
4	Kt-KB3 / Kt-R3		P-Q4 / Kt-K2 (4)	P-Q4 / Kt-KB3	PxP en pass / BxP	PxQBP / BxP
5	P-KKt3 / B-K2	P-QKt3	B-Q3 / Kt-Kt3	P-KB4 / P-Q4	P-Q4 / P-QB4	Kt-QB3 / Q-B2!
6	B-Kt2 / Castles	B-Kt2 / Kt-B4	Kt-KB3 / Kt-B3	B-Q3 / Kt-B3	PxP / Q-R4ch	B-KB4? / Q-Kt3
7	P-Q3 / P-B3	P-B3 / R-QKtsq	Kt-B3 / Kt-Kt5	Kt-KB3 / B-Q3	Kt-B3 / QxBP	Q-Q2 / BxPch
8	PxP / BxP	Q-K2 / B-Kt2	B-QB4 / P-QB3	P-B3 / Q-B2	B-Q3 / Kt-KB3	QxB / QxP
9	Castles / Kt-B2	P-Q3 / B-K2	Kt-K4 / B-B2	P-KKt3 / B-Q2	Q-K2 / B-Q2	K-Q2 / QxR
10	P-B3 / R-Ktsq	Kt-Q2 / P-Q4	Castles / Castles	QKt-Q2 / P-KR3	Kt-B3 / Kt-B3	Kt-Kt5 / Kt-QR3
11	Kt-R3 / P-QKt3	PxP en pass / KtxQP	R-Ksq / Kt-Q4	Kt-K5 / BxKt?	B-K3 / Q-QR4	Kt-Q6ch / K-Bsq
12	Kt-B2 / B-Kt2	Castles / Castles	Kt-B5 / Kt-R5	BPxB / Kt-KKtsq	CastlesKR / B-B4	BxKt / PxB
13	Kt-K3 / P-Q4	R-Qsq / Q-Bsq	Kt-K5 / Kt-B4	Castles / KKt-K2	P-QR3 / BxBch	Q-B5 / Kt-K2
14	Kt-Kt4 / P-K4	Kt-Bsq / R-Qsq	P-QB3 / BxKt	Q-R5 / P-KKt3	QxB / Kt-KKt5	Kt-K2 / QxR
15	KtxBch / PxKt	B-K3 / B-R3	RxB / Kt-B3	Q-R4 / R-R2	Q-Q2 / Q-QB4ch	PxP / PxP
16	Kt-R4 / Kt-K2	Q-QB2 / Kt-Ksq	R-Ksq / P-KR3	Kt-B3 / Castles	K-Rsq / Q-K6	B-R6ch (8) / K-Ktsq
17	PxP / PxP	B-B2 / R-Kt2	Q-B3 / Kt-Q4	Kt-Kt5 / R-Kt2 (A)	QxQ / KtxQ	Q-Q4 / QxRP
18	Q-Kt4ch / K-Rsq	Kt-K3 / QR-Q2	B-Kt3 / P-QKt3	QxP / QR-Ktsq	KR-Ksq / Kt-KKt5	B-B4 / Q-R4
19	Q-R5 / Q-Ksq	Kt-Ksq / Kt-B3	Kt-Q3 / B-R3	RxP / Kt-...	Kt-K4 / K-R2	QxBP / Kt-Q4
20	P-Q4+	Q-K2 — / B-Kt2—	Kt-K5+	BxKt+	P-R3+ (6)	Q-Q8ch / K-Kt2 (9)

For Notes see page 25.

FRENCH DEFENCE.

	7	8	9	10	11	12
	Vienna 1882 Congress.	Vienna 1882 Congress.	Vienna 1882 Congress.	Toronto, 1884.	Nuremberg 1883 Congress.	New Orleans, 1883.
	Weiss Schwarz	Rosenthal Noa	Wittek Mason	Zukertort Ald. Judd	Fritz Mason	Zukertort McConnell
1	P-K4 / P-K3					
2	P-Q4 / P-Q4					
3	Kt-QB3 / Kt-KB3					B-Kt5 (19)
4	PxP / PxP				B-KK5 / B-K2	PxP / BxKtch
5	Kt-B3 / B-Q3				BxKt / BxB	PxB / PxP
6	B-Q3 / Castles		Kt-B3		Kt-B3 / Castles (18)	Kt-B3 / B-Kt5
7	Castles / B-KKt5	P-B3	P-QR3 / B-KKt5	Castles / Castles	B-Q3 / P-QKt3	B-K2 / Kt-KB3
8	P-KR3 / B-R4	Kt-K2 / Q-B2	B-K3 / Castles	B-KKt5 / B-K2	P-KR4! / B-Kt2	Castles (20) / Kt-K5
9	P-KKt4 / B-Kt3	Kt-Kt3 / B-KKt5	P-R3 / B-K3	R-Ksq / P-KR3	P-K5 / B-K2	Q-Q3 / Castles
10	P-Kt5 (10) / Kt-R4	P-KR3 / B-K3	Castles / Q-Q2	B-K3 (16) / Kt-QKt5	BxPch / KxB	P-B4 / P-QB3
11	KtxP / P-QB3	Kt-Kt5 / R-Ksq	R-Ksq / KR-Ksq	B-KBsq / B-KB4	Kt-Kt5ch / K-Kt3!	PxP / PxP
12	Kt-B3 (11) / Kt-Q2	P-KB4 / P-KR3	B-KKt5 / K-Rsq	R-Bsq / Kt-K5	Kt-K2 / BxKt	P-QB4 / Kt-QB3
13	Kt-K2?(12) / R-Ksq	KtxB / RxKt	Q-Q2 / Kt-KR4	KtxKt / PxKt	PxB / P-KB4	R-Ktsq? / B-B4
14	K-Kt2 / Kt-Bsq	Kt-B5 / QKt-Q2	B-Bsq (14) / P-B3	P-QR3 / B-Kt5 (17)	KtPxP en p / R-Rsq	PxP / Kt-Kt6
15	Kt-Kt3 / Kt-B5ch	KtxB / QxKt	B-K3 / P-B4	PxKt / PxKt	Kt-B4ch / K-B2	Q-Qsq / KtxBch
16	BxKt / KBxB	P-B3 / Kt-K5	Kt-K2 / Kt-B3	PxP / B-R4	Q-Kt4 / RxRch	QxKt / BxR
17	P-KR4 / Q-Q2	P-B5 / R-K2	B-B4 / Kt-K5	P-B3 / B-Q3	K-Q2 / PxP	PxKt / PxP
18	P-B3 / Q-Kt5	B-KB4 / Q-B3	Q-Bsq / Q-K2	B-Kt2 / Q-R5	Q-Kt6ch / K-K2	B-R3 / R-Ksq
19	R-Rsq / BxKt	Q-Kt4 / QR-Ksq	BxB / PxB	P-R3 / Q-B3	Q-Kt7ch / K-Ksq	Q-B4 / B-K5
20	PxB / R-K6+	QR-Qsq / P-R3 (13)	Kt-R2 / Q-R5 (15)	P-Kt5 / P-R3+	Q-Kt8ch+	Kt-K5 / RxKt+

For Notes see page 390

FRENCH DEFENCE.

	13	14	15	16	17	18
	Vienna 1882 Congress. Paulsen Mason		Vienna 1882 Congress. Tschigorin Noa	Vienna 1882 Congress. Tschigorin Fleissig	Toronto, 1883. Zukertort Kittson	Vienna 1882 Congress. Mackenzie Noa
1	P-K4 / P-K3					
2	P-Q4 / P-Q4					
3	P-K5 / P-QB4	PxP / PxP				
4	P-QB3 / Kt-QB3	Kt-KB3 / Kt-KB3				
5	Kt-B3 / B-Q2	B-Q3 / B-Q3				
6	B-Q3 / Q-Kt3	Castles / Castles				B-KKt5 / Q-K2ch
7	PxP / BxP	Kt-B3 / P-B3			P-QKt3 / B-KKt5(24)	B-K2 / P-KR3
8	Castles / Q-B2	Kt-K2 / Q-B2	B-KKt5 / B-KKt5		P-B4 / P-B3	B-R4 / B-KKt5
9	B-KB4 / KKt-K2	Kt-Kt3 / B-K3	P-KR3 / B-R4		QKt-Q2 / QKt-Q2	QKt-Q2 / QKt-Q2
10	P-QKt4 / B-Kt3	P-Kt3 (21)	P-KKt4(22) / B-Kt3		Q-B2 / R-Ksq	P-B3 / CastlesQR
11	P-QR4 / P-QR3		Kt-K5 / Q-B2	QKt-Q2	B-Kt2 / R-QBsq	Castles / P-KKt4
12	R-Ksq / Kt-Kt3		P-B4 / BxB	P-B4 / Q-Kt3	P-B5 / B-Ktsq	B-Kt3 / BxB
13	B-Kt3 / QKt-K2		QxB / QKt-Q2	KtxKt / KtxKt	P-Kt4 / BxKt	RPxB / Kt-K5
14	P-R4 / P-R3		QR-Ksq / QR-Ksq	P-B5? / QxPch	KtxB / Kt-Bsq	KtxKt / PxKt
15	Q-Kt3 / R-QBsq		Q-B5 / R-K3	K-Kt2 / P-B3	P-QR4 / Kt-K5	Kt-Q2 / P-KR4!
16	R-R2 / B-R2		KtxKt / QxKt	PxB / PxB	P-Kt5 / Q-B2	BxB / PxB
17	P-KR5 / Kt-Bsq		BxKt / PxB	Kt-K2 / Q-Kt3	KR-Ksq / Kt-Kt4	QxP / P-K6
18	R-B2 / P-QKt4		Kt-K2 / Q-K2 (23)	B-B5 / Q-K6	Kt-K5 / P-B3	KR-Ksq / P-KB4 (25)
19	PxP / BxP		R-B2 / R-Ksq	R-B3 / Q-K4	P-B4 / PxKt	
20	BxB / PxB+		P-KR4 / R-K5+	PxPch / K-Rsq+	QPxP / Kt-K5+	

For Notes see page 25.

Notes, to pages 22, 23, and 24.

(1) One of several innovations tried by Mr Steinitz at this Congress.

(2) Mr Sellman would prefer 2 P-Q4 or 2 P-KB3.

(3) Mr Max Judd suggests for Black 3 P-KKt4, with the view of isolating White's KP.

(4) Not good, the Kt should have gone to B3.

(A) Black should have Castled at his 11th move.

(5) Novelty for novelty.

(6) The game ran up to nearly 60 moves, White winning at last by a slight advantage in position.

(7) Mr Gunsberg and the London "CHESS PLAYER'S CHRONICLE" approve of this reply. Should White take the P, Black retakes with the Kt, thereby having won a move. If White support his exposed K P, Black further develops his attack on the advanced position.

(8) It is said that this move cost Steinitz £70, and a division of the first honors at the Vienna Congress. The game is one of those fought after the last round, to decide the tie, the result being another and final tie.

(9) Continued 21 Q-R5 21 KtxB, 22 Q-B3ch 22 P-K4, 23 KtxKt 23 Q-Kt4, 24 P-Kt3 24 R-Bsq, 25 Kt-K4 25 Q-K2, 26 Kt-Q5 26 Q-K3, 27 Kt-B7 27 Q-R3ch, and White resigned.

(10) Mr Steinitz said this is new, and it is strange that the simple combination of the last two moves, which wins a Pawn, should not have been adopted before. Though Black obtains some counter attack, this does not outweigh the material loss. (See Diagram on page 21.)

(11) Best, to prevent Kt-B5.

(12) An error. It was here important to gain a move, which could have been effected by Kt-K4, compelling an exchange of Pieces or the retreat of the Bishop.

(13) White won in an end game, having two Bishops against two Knights.

(14) Loss of time. Mr Sellman says Kt-K5 would have relieved him at once from the threatened pressure.

(15) Black won.

(16) Dr I Ryall says B-R4, is better. The text move confines White's Pieces, and apparently gives the attack to Black. ·

(17) PxKt would be better, winning a Pawn with a good position.

(18) Premature.

(19) This move, with the capture of Kt that follows, is condemned by the authorities; but Mr McConnell prefers it to 3 Kt-KB3 for the defence.

(20) B-R3 would hamper Black's game.

(21) A new idea, played successfully by Dr Zukertort at the London Congress. Mr Freeborough says this move of White is to be recommended, as it enables him to conduct on both wings, operations that may supplement each other.

(22) A line of attack first prominently brought into notice at this tournament, by the Vienna players.

(23) Black takes the attack from this point.

(24) This move was adopted in reply to 7 Kt-B3, in a series of games between Messrs Judd and Kittson, of the Hamilton (Ontario) Chess Club, and they are of the opinion that 7 B-KKt5 is Black's best move.

(25) Mr Sellman says this is to the point. Should White now play 19 QxBP, Black responds with 19 KR-Bsq, and the following would be the best moves in continuation : 20 RxP 20 QxR, 21 QxKtch 21 RxQ, 22 PxQ, and Black comes out with the exchange against two clear Pawns; the chances appearing to be about equal. White eventually won, Black letting victory slip through his fingers.

THE SCOTCH GÁMBIT.

NO very prominent novelty in this Gambit has been presented within the last three years. The Opening, as generally played now, is not a Gambit, the Pawn being recaptured on White's fourth move. Nearly all variations of the Scotch lead to highly interesting, and often brilliant positions, and it is a game prolific of counter attacks for Black. The neglect of such Openings in tournaments and matches, is typical of the state of affairs which induced Mr John Ruskin to write recently to an English periodical, "Chess, I urge pupils to learn, and enjoy it myself, to the point of its becoming a temptation to waste of time,- often very difficult to resist; and I have really serious thoughts of publishing a selection of favorite old games, by Chess players of real genius and imagination, as opposed to the stupidity, called Chess playing in modern days. Pleasant 'play,' truly! in which the opponents sit calculating and analysing for twelve hours, tire each other nearly into apoplexy or idiocy, and end in a draw, or a victory by an odd Pawn." While Mr Ruskin does not quite do justice to the modern time limit system in set encounters, he will find a multitude to agree with him, that the favorite old games are more interesting than those of the present day.

$$1 \frac{\text{P-K4}}{\text{P-K4}} \quad 2 \frac{\text{Kt-KB3}}{\text{Kt-QB3}} \quad 3 \frac{\text{P-Q4}}{\text{PxP}}$$

Position after Black's 3rd move.

BLACK.

WHITE.

SCOTCH GAMBIT.

(See Diagram on page 26.)

	1	2	3	4	5	6
	Match 1882 London.	Coml Gaz Cor Tourney 1883.	Hamilton 1882 Tourney.	Nuremberg 1883 Congress.	Challenge Cup M'chester 1884.	St. George's v Bristol, &c. 84
	Blackburne Mackenzie	Ferris Braithwaite	Braithwaite Henderson	Blackburne Gunsberg	Von Zabern Jones	Wayte Fedden
4	KtxP					
	B-B4					
5	B-K3					
	Q-B3					
6	P-QB3					
	KKt-K2					
7	Kt-B2 (1)	B-QB4		Q-Q2	P-KB4	
	B-Kt3 (2)	Kt-K4		KtxKt	P-Q4	
8	QKt-R3 (3)	B-Kt3		PxKt	P-K5	
	Q-Kt3	Castles		B-Kt3	Q-R3	Q-R5ch
9	P-B3	Castles		Kt-B3	Q-Q2	P-KKt3
	Kt-Qsq	P-Q3		P-KR3	KtxKt (8)	Q-Kt5
10	Q-Q2	P-KR3		B-QB4	PxKt	B-K2 (10)
	Kt-K3	B-Q2		P-Q3	B-Kt3	Q-R6
11	Kt-B4	Kt-Q2		CastlesKR	B-Q3	B-B3
	P-Q3	KKt-Kt3		Kt-B3	B-KB4	B-Kt3
12	KtxB	P-KB4		Kt-Q5	Kt-B3	Kt-R3
	RPxKt	Kt-B3		Q-Kt3	R-Qsq	P-KR4
13	B-QB4	P-B5		KR-Ksq	CastlesKR	Q-Q2
	Castles	KKt-K2	KKt-K4	Castles	Castles	KtxKt
14	P-KKt4	Kt(Q2)-B3	Q-R5	QR-Bsq	P-QKt4	PxKt
	Kt-B3	Kt-K4	P-KKt3	K-Rsq	Q-Kt3	Q-Q2
15	CastlQR (4)	K-Rsq	PxP	Kt-B4	B-K2	CastQR(11)
	Kt-K4	P-KR3	QxP	Q-R2	P-QR4	Q-B3ch
16	B-K2	KtxKt	Q-R4	P-QKt4	P-QR3	K-Ktsq
	Kt-B4	PxKt (6)	K-Kt2	P-B4	Kt-B3	B-KB4ch
17	BxKt	Kt-K6	B-Qsq	P-K5	Kt-R4	K-Rsq
	KtPxB	BxB!	P-B4	P-Kt4?	B-R2 (9)	Q-Kt3
18	P-KB4	KtxR	B-R5	PxP	P-Kt5	R-QBsq
	Kt-B3	B-B3	Q-B3	PxKt	Kt-K2	P-QB3
19	P-B5	Kt-Q7	B-Kt5+	BxP	QxP	KR-Ksq
	Q-B3	Q-Kt4		PxP	B-K5	K-Q2
20	P-Kt5	KtxP+		BxP	B-B3+	Kt-Ktsq—
	Q-K4 (5)			B-Q2 (7)		B-Kt5 —

For Notes see page 29.

SCOTCH GAMBIT.

(See Diagram on page 26.)

	7 New Orleans, 1882. Mackenzie Maurian	8 Nuremberg 1883 Congress. Paulsen Leffman	9 Vienna 1882 Congress. Fleissig Zukertort	10 Vienna 1882 Congress. Paulsen Winawer	11 Match 1883 Havana. Golmayo Steinitz	12 London 1883 Congress. Rosenthal Bird
4	KtxP / P-Q4 (12)	Kt-B3	B-B4	Q-R5 (18)		B-QB4 / B-B4
5	B-QKt5 / Q-Q3	Kt-QB3 / B-Kt5	B-K3 (16) / Q-B3	Kt-Kt5 / B-Kt5ch (19	Q-KPch	Castles / P-Q3
6	PxP / QxP	KtxKt / BxKtch	P-QB3 / KKt-K2	P-QB3 / B-B4	B-K2 / B-Kt5ch	P-B3 / B-KKt5
7	KtxKt (13) / Q-K5ch	PxB / QPxKt	Kt-B2 / P-Q3	Q-K2 / B-Kt3	B-Q2 / K-Qsq	Q-Kt3 / BxKt
8	Q-K2 / QxQch	B-Q3 / B-Kt5	Kt-Q2 / Kt-K4	B-K3 (20) / Q-Qsq	Castles / BxB	BxPch / K-Bsq
9	KxQ / P-QR3	P-B3 / B-K3	BxB / PxB	BxB / RPxB	QxB / P-QR3	PxB (24) / Kt-B3
10	B-R4 / B-Q2	Castles / Q-Q2	Kt-K3 / B-K3	P-KKt3 / P-Q3	KKt-B3 / Q-KR5	B-Q5 / Q-Bsq
11	B-B4 / P-QKt4	B-K3 / P-KR4	Q-R4ch / P-B3	B-Kt2 / KKt-K2	Kt-R3 / P-QKt4	B-K6 / Q-Ksq
12	Kt-K5 / PxB	P-QR4 / P-R5	B-K2 / CastlesKR	Kt-Q2 / Castles	B-B3 / Q-R3	B-B5 / B-Kt3
13	KtxB / KxKt	Q-Ktsq / P-QKt3	CastlesKR / Kt(Q2)-Kt3	Kt-B3 / B-Kt5	QR-Qsq(21) / QxQ	B-B4 / Q-R4
14	R-Qsqch / K-B3	P-R5 / K-K2	P-KKt3 / KR-Qsq	P-KR3 / BxKt	RxQ / KKt-K2	Kt-Q2 / R-Ksq
15	Kt-B3 / R-Ksqch	R-Qsq / P-B4	Q-B2 / B-R6?	BxB / P-B4	Kt-Q5 / R-QKtsq	Q-Qsq / Q-B2
16	K-Bsq / P-R6	P-KB4 / Q-B3	P-KB4 / BxR	PxP / RxP	R-Ksq / P-Q3	K-Rsq / Kt-K2
17	PxP / BxP	P-K5 (15) / Kt-Kt5	PxKt / KtxP	B-K4 / R-B3	QR-K2 / B-K3	B-R3 / PxP
18	Kt-Q5 / Kt-B3	B-QBsq / P-R6	RxB / Q-K3	CastlesKR / Q-Q2	Kt-KB4 / Kt-Q5 (22)	PxP / KtxP
19	KtxP / R-K5	B-Bsq / KtxP	Kt(Q2)-B4 / P-QKt4	B-Kt2 / QR-KBsq	R-K4 / KtxBch	PxKt / QxB
20	B-Kt3 / P-QR4 (14)	Q-Kt5 / Kt-B6ch!+	KtxKt+ (17	QR-Qsq+	PxKt / Kt-B4 (23)	B-Q7 / R-Qsq

Game was drawn.

Notes, to pages 27 and 28.

(1) The usual continuation for White here is B-QB4, B-QKt5, or Q-Q2.

(2) P-Q3 may also be played. Mr Steinitz commended the Captain's move, as he obtained an open Rook's file later on, when the Bishops were exchanged.

(3) Mr Steinitz would have preferred Kt-Q2. Black is able to defeat White's intention to exchange the B, and play Kt-Kt5.

(4) White should rather have continued the advance on the K side with P-KR4.

(5) Continued 21 B-B3 21 RxP, and Black won. Mr Steinitz attributes the loss of the game to White's failure to push on his KRP.

(6) If 16 QxKt, 17 Kt-B3, and White wins a Piece.

(7) Continued 21 R-K7 ! 21 Q-Kt3, 22 RxB 22 KR-Qsq, 23 B-K5ch 23 KtxB, 24 PxKt 24 RxR, 25 QxR, and White won. In this game White made the best development in opening. His 21st move brought about a winning end game.

(8) The approved move is BxKt.

(9) Losing a Pawn. But if the B had not been moved, White's Kt would have taken it, greatly weakening Black's centre.

(10) Rev W Wayte says Q-Q2, followed by B-Kt2 seems equally good.

(11) Better have Castled with KR, says the same authority, and if 15 P-R5, 16 P-KKt4. Black's development then would have been extremely difficult, and White would have had time for a decisive advance of the Pawns. The text play gave Black an opportunity to clear his game.

(12) An experimental move by Mr Maurian.

(13) White seems certain to win a Piece, but Black saves it ingeniously.

(14) Continued 21 R-Q3 21 B-B4, 22 R-QB3 22 K-Kt3, 23 P-QR3 23 Kt-Q2, 24 R-Ktsqch 24 K-B3, 25 Kt-R6 25 KR-Ksq, 26 P-B3 26 R-Q5, 27 B-B2 27 R-Q4, 28 P-QR4 28 KR-K4, 29 P-Kt4 29 P-Kt4, 30 R-Kt5 30 P-R4, 31 RxP 31 PxP, 32 PxP 32 P-B4, and this move permitted White to exchange off all the Pieces, after which one of his passed Pawns won.

(15) The "Schachzeitung" says this is hasty, and that P-B5 would have been stronger.

(16) This continuation is now preferred to 5 KtxKt, which soon results in an even end game.

(17) Black could not extricate himself from the results of his 15th move. He resigned on the 36th.

(18) A move not much played recently.

(19) Unusual.

(20) Taking advantage of the novelty.

(21) Not as good as QxQ.

(22) Sacrificing a Pawn for a strong attack.

(23) The remaining moves in this interesting game were 21 KtxB 21 PxKt, 22 RxP 22 P-Kt5, 23 Kt-B4 23 Kt-Q5, 24 R(K6)-K3 24 KtxQBP, 25 Kt-R5 25 R-Kt4, 26 Kt-B6ch 26 K-Q2, 27 Kt-R7 (the Kt cannot get out) 27 R-Kt4ch, and White resigns.

(24) Better, says "Land and Water," than BxKt, but this is not saying much.

THE GIUOCO PIANO.

ALTHOUGH, as indicated by the " Synopsis," the drift of analysis in this Opening is in favor of the defence, the debut has been frequently played during the last three years in important contests.   At this time 4 P-Q3 is considered the best continuation of the attack, Mr Steinitz and M Rosenthal, among other masters, preferring this line.

The " Jerome Gambit "—4 BxPch—involves an unsound sacrifice ; but it is not an attack to be trifled with.   The defence requires study, and is somewhat difficult.   We give the fullest analysis of this American invention that has yet been in print.   The author is Mr S A Charles, Cincinnati, Ohio.

———

$$1 \ \frac{\text{P-K4}}{\text{P-K4}} \qquad 2 \ \frac{\text{Kt-KB3}}{\text{Kt-QB3}} \qquad 3 \ \frac{\text{B-B4}}{\text{B-B4}}$$

Position after Black's 3rd move.

BLACK.

WHITE.

GIUOCO PIANO.

(See Diagram on page 30.)

	1	2	3	4	5	6
	Vienna 1882 Congress.	New Orleans 1884.	New Orleans 1884.	London 1883 Congress.	3rd French Nat Tour '83.	Vienna 1882 Congress.
	Mason Winawer	Maurian Zukertort	Maurian Zukertort	Blackburne Tschigorin	Goudjou De Rivière	Bird Fleissig
4	P-Q3	Kt-B3		P-B3		
	P-Q3			Kt-B3	P-Q3 (11)	
5	B-K3	B-K3		P-Q3	P-Q3	P-QKt4
	B-Kt3 (1)	B-Kt3		P-Q3	Kt-B3	B-Kt3
6	QKt-Q2	P-B3	QKt-Q2	B-K3	B-K3	Q-Kt3
	P-KR3	P-Q3	P-Q3	B-Kt3	B-Kt3	Q-K2
7	Kt-Bsq	Kt-Q2	Kt-Bsq	QKt-Q2	QKt-Q2	P-QR4
	Kt-B3	Kt-K2	Kt-K2	B-K3	B-K3	P-QR4
8	P-KR3	Kt-Bsq	Kt-Kt3	Q-K2	Q-K2 (12)	P-Kt5
	Kt-K2	P-B3	P-KR3	Q-Q2	Q-K2	Kt-Qsq
9	Kt-Kt3	Q-Kt3	Q-Q2	B-QKt5	CastlesKR	P-Q3
	P-B3	Castles	P-B3	P-QR3	P-KR3	Kt-KB3
10	B-Kt3	Q-B2	P-B3	B-R4	KR-Ksq	QKt-Q2
	BxB (2)	P-KR3	P-Kt4	BxB	P-Kt4	Kt-K3
11	PxB	Kt-Kt3	P-Q4	PxB	KBxB	Kt-Bsq
	Q-Kt3	Kt-Kt3	Q-B2	CastlesKR	QxB (13)	Kt-B4
12	Q-Q2	CastlesKR	R-Qsq	P-Q4	Kt-Bsq	Q-B2
	P-QR4	P-Q4	Kt-Kt5	P-QKt4	Kt-K2	B-K3
13	P-B3	B-Kt3? (4)	P-KR3	B-B2	Kt-Kt3	Kt-K3
	P-R5	BxB	KtxB	B-Kt5	Kt-Kt3	CastlesKR
14	B-Qsq	PxB	QxKt (6)	CastlesKR	Kt-B5	BxB
	B-K3	PxP	Kt-Kt3	QR-Ksq	CastlesQR	PxB
15	Castles	PxP	Kt-R5	P-QR4	BxB! (14)	Kt-B4
	Q-B2	Q-Kt3	Kt-B5	Kt-K2	Kt-B5 (15)	QKt-Q2
16	Kt-R4	QR-Ksq	KtxKt	RFxP	Q-B2	KtxB
	P-QKt4	Kt-Kt5	KtPxKt	RPxP	RPxB	KtxKt
17	B-B2	Q-Bsq	Q-Q2	R-R5	P-KKt3	Q-Kt3
	P-B4	Kt-B5	R-KKtsq (7	P-B3	Kt-Kt3	QKt-Q2
18	Kt(Kt3-B5	B-B2	K-Bsq	KR-Rsq	P-Q4	B-K3
	BxKt	B-K3	R-Kt3	Kt-Kt3	Kt-Q2?	P-QKt3
19	KtxB	P-Kt3	Kt-R4	R-R7	P-Q5	CastlesKR
	KtxKt	QR-Qsq	R-B3 (8	Q-Bsq	Q-B3	K-Rsq
20	RxKt	KtxP	Q-K2	P-Q5+ (10)	Kt-Q2+	QR-Ksq
	Kt-Q2 (3)	KtxKtP (5)	B-Q2 (9)			Kt-R4+

For Notes see page 33.

GIUOCO PIANO.

(See Diagram on page 30.)

	7	8	9	10	11	12
	Amsterdam 1882 Tourney	Match 1882 London	Correspond. Game 1874.		Canada.	Bristol, &c. v S George's 84.
	Veraart Loman	Blackburne Mackenzie	Marino, Ill. Cincinnati		Ryall Narraway	Fedden Wayte
4	P-B3					Castles
	Kt-B3					Kt-B3
5	P-Q3		P-Q4		B-Q5 (28)	P-Q3
	P-Q3		PxP		Castles	P-Q3
6	B-K3		P-K5?	PxP	BxKt	B-KKt5(29)
	B-Kt3		P-Q4	B-Kt5ch	QPxB	P-KR3
7	QKt-Q2 (16)		B-QKt5	B-Q2	KtxP	B-R4
	Kt-K2	B-K3	Kt-K5	BxBch	KtxP	P-KKt4
8	P-KR3	Q-B2 (21)	BxKtch	QKtxB	P-Q4	B-KKt3
	Kt-Kt3	KBxB	PxB	KtxKP	B-Q3	P-KR4 (30)
9	P-Q4	PxB	PxP	KtxKt	Castles	KtxKtP
	PxP	Kt-KKt5	B-Kt3	P-Q4	P-KR3	P-R5
10	PxP	BxB	Kt-B3	KKtKt5(24)	P-KB4	KtxP
	P-Q4	KtxKP	P-KB4	Castles	P-KB3	PxB (31)
11	B-Q3 (17)	BxPch	Castles	Q-R5 (25)	Kt-Kt6	KtxQ (32)
	PxP	KxB	Castles	B-B4 (26)	R-B2	B-KKt5
12	KtxP	Q-Kt3ch	B-B4	KtxRP	P-B5	Q-Q2 (33)
	Castles	K-K2	B-Kt2	BxQKt	P-B4	Kt-Q5
13	Q-B2 (18)	K-B2	Kt-QR4	KtxR	Q-Kt4	Kt-B3 (34)
	KtxKt	Kt-KKt5ch	P-Kt4	PxB+ (27)	Kt-Kt4	
14	BxKt	K-K2	KtxB		P-KR4	
	P-KB4	Q-Q2	RPxKt		Kt-R2	
15	Q-B4ch	QR-KBsq	B-Bsq!		Kt-Q2	
	K-Rsq	KR-KBsq	B-R3 (22)		PxP	
16	B-B2	P-KR3	R-Ksq		QxP	
	P-B5	Kt-B3	P-Kt5		P-Kt3	
17	BxKt	P-Kt4	Kt-Q2		K-Rsq	
	PxB(K6)	P-QKt3	KtxP		B-Kt2	
18	PxP (19)	Kt-B4	KxKt!		Kt-Kt3	
	PxB	P-Kt3	Q-R5ch		P-B4	
19	CastlesKR	Kt-K3	K-Ktsq		Q-KKt4	
	Q-Ksq (20)	QR-Ksq	P-B5!		Q-B2	
20	Kt-K5	R-B2	Kt-B3		B-B4+	
	RxRch +	Kt-KR4+	PxKt (23)			

NOTES, to pages 31 and 32.

(1) The latest (sixth) edition of the German " Handbuch " gives BxB, and an analysis to show that by this move Black obtains the better game.

(2) Castling would be better.

(3) Not as good as CastlesKR. White made a centre attack, and won on the 51st move.

(4) He should have exchanged Bishops.

(5) Continued 21 KxKt 21 KtxKt, 22 R-Qsq 22 Kt-Kt5, 23 R-Q4 23 P-QB4, 24 RxR. This last move of White's is much inferior to R-Qsq, when if 24 P-B5, 25 R-Q4 25 PxP, 26 PxP, and, as Black cannot capture the P, White remains with a fair game. The game was won by Black, on the 34th move.

(6) If 14 PxKt Black rejoins 14 PxP, and White cannot retake without losing a Piece, by 15 P-Q4

(7) Mr Maurian says that 17 B-Q2, preparatory to Castling, would give Black a slight superiority.

(8) If 19 R-Kt2, or Ktsq, White would probably gain an advantage by 20 PxP, followed by Q-Q6.

(9) Continued 21 Q-R5 21 Castles, 22 PxP (capturing BP would result in losing QP) 22 PxP, 23 Kt-B3 23 B-K3, 24 RxRch 24 QxR, 25 KtxP 25 P-B6? and Black lost. He could have drawn by 25 BxB.

(10) Mr Blackburne won on the 44th move. His success was mainly due to his attack on Black's centre, which began on White's 9th move.

(11) M Rosenthal prefers Kt-B3, and P-Q4 for White's next move.

(12) Inferior to B-Kt3.

(13) This move allows the White Kt to take up a strong position at KB5. Black could have obtained a favorable position by 11 PxB, followed by CastlesQR.

(14) The Pawns on the Q side can now advance.

(15) Worse than useless, as it drives the Q to a better position.

(16) This move is not considered as strong as formerly.

(17) The Berlin " Sonntagsblatt " prefers 11 PxP, followed by 12 Q-Kt3.

(18) Castles would be better.

(19) White is compelled to sacrifice a Piece, as a consequence of his 13th move, otherwise he ould lose the chance of Castling, and have to bear a strong attack.

(20) Not so strong as B-KB4.

(21) In Mr Steinitz's opinion the Q would be better posted at K2.

(22) Intending to sacrifice the Kt.

(23) White's 20th move is bad; R-Bsq or K2 giving the only chance for a draw. The game continued 21 PxP 21 K-Rsq, 22 K-Rsq 22 R-KKtsq, 23 Q-Q2 23 R-Kt3, 24 R-KKtsq, and Black announced mate in eight moves.

(24) In a communication to the London "Chess Monthly," for March 1883, Mr A A Bowley says, this ingenious move results to Black's advantage, if he replies to it 10 Castles, as in the text. If Black replies 10 B-B4 he does not fare so well, the play continuing 11 KtxBP 11 KxKt, 12 Kt-Kt3.

(25) If 11 KtxRP, Black obtains a superior game by R-Ksq.

(26) The only move. If 11 P-KR3, 12 KtxBP+.

(27) Black remains with two minor Pieces for the R, as the White Kt cannot escape.

(28) Dr I Ryall, Hamilton, Ont., says he has a liking for this move, after testing it in many games. Though not always successful, it leads to very interesting positions.

(29) Premature.

(30) First played by Steinitz against Dubois, Congress of 1862, p 102. Dubois did not venture 9 KtxKtP, but defended himself by 9 P-KR4.

(31) Steinitz contemplated Q-K2 at this point, but Lowenthal afterward showed, C P C 1868-9, p 162, that Black can give his opponent the choice of Q or R.

(32) If 11 KtxR 11 Q-K2, 12 B-B7ch (or A) 12 K-Qsq, 13 Kt-Q2 13 BxPch, 14 K-Rsq 14 Kt-KKt5, 15 Kt-B3 15 Q-B3, winning. (A) If 12 Kt-B7 12 BxPch, 13 RxB 13 PxRch, 14 KxP 14 Kt-KKt5ch, 15 Kt-Kt3 15 Q-B3, 16 Q-B3 16 Q-Kt2 and wins.

(33) Q-Ksq comes to the same thing. If Kt-B7, Black may play RxP.

(34) Black announced mate in seven moves.

GIUOCO PIANO. JEROME GAMBIT.

$$1 \; \frac{\text{P-K4}}{\text{P-K4}} \quad 2 \; \frac{\text{Kt-KB3}}{\text{Kt-QB3}} \quad 3 \; \frac{\text{B-B4}}{\text{B-B4}} \quad 4 \; \frac{\text{BxPch}}{\text{KxB}}$$

	1	2	3	4	5	6
5	KtxPch / KtxKt!					K-Bsq?
6	Q-R5ch / K-K3! (1)			P-Q4 / BxP		KtxKt / QPxKt (8)
7	Q-B5ch / K-Q3	P-KB4 / P-Q3	Castles / P-Q3! (5)	QxB / P-Q3!	Q-B3	Castles / Kt-B3
8	P-KB4 (2) / Q-B3	Q-R3ch (4) / K-K2	Kt-B3 / Kt-KB3	Kt-B3 (7) / Kt-KB3	Q-Qsq / P-Q3	Q-B3 (9) / Q-Q5
9	PxKtch / QxP	P-B5 / BxP	Q-Qsq / Kt-Q6 (6)	B-Kt5 / P-R3!	Castles / P-KKt3	P-Q3 / B-KKt5
10	Q-B3 / Kt-B3	PxB / Q-Q2	PxKt / K-B2	BxKt / QxB	P-KB4 / Kt-B3	Q-Kt3 / B-Q3
11	P-Q3 / K-B3	P-Q4 / BxP	Kt-K2 / B-Kt3	CastlesQR / B-K3		P-QB3+
12	Kt-B3 / P-Q3 (3)	Q-R4ch / Kt-KB3	K-Rsq / Kt-Kt5	K-Ktsq / Kt-B5		
13	P-KR3 / Q-R4	QxB / QxP+	P-Q4 / KtxRP	Q-Q3 / P-QKt4		
14	Q-Kt3 / B-K3		KxKt / Q-R5ch	P-B4 / KtxP		
15	Kt-K2 / QR-KBsq		K-Ktsq / QxKP	KxKt / P-Kt5!		
16	Kt-B4 / KtxP		P-Q3 / Q-Kt5			
17	PxKt / Q-K4		B-K3 / P-Q4			
18	Q-Q3 / B-B4+		P-B3 / Q-K3			
19			B-B2 / P-B3+			

(1) If 6 Kt-Kt3?, 7 Q-Q5ch 7 K-Ksq, 8 QxB 8 P-Q3, 9 Q-B3 9 Kt-B3, 10 P-Q3.

(2) If 8 P-Q4 8 BxP, 9 Kt-R3 9 K-B3+

(3) 12 P-Q4 also looks good.

(4) If 8 P-B5ch 8 K-Q2, 9 P-Q3 9 Kt-KB3, 10 Q-Qsq 10 KtxKP+.

(5) If 7 P-KKt3, 8 Q-R3ch 8 Kmoves, 9 Q-QB3. If 7 Q-B3, 8 P-QKt4 8 Q-Kt3, 9 Q-R3ch 9 K-Q3, 10 PxBch 10 K-B3, 11 P-Q4+.

(6) If 9 K-B2, 10 P-Q4 10 B-KKt5, 11 P-B3 (if 11 Q-Q2 11 B-Kt3, 12 PxKt 12 PxP!) 11 KtxBPch, 12 PxKt 12 B-R6+. 9 Kt-B3+.

(7) If 8 Castles 8 Kt-KB3, 9 P-KB4 9 Kt-B3.

(8) If 6 KtPxKt, 7 P-Q4.

(9) If 8 P-Q4 8 B-KKt5, 9 Q-Ksq 9 K-B2.

TWO KNIGHTS' DEFENCE.

THIS Opening leads to intricate and daring counter attacks, and analysis has not yet determined whether the advantage in the middle game inclines to White or Black. Such being the case, it is an Opening to be encouraged, and yet it is one occupying very few pages in the books of Chess Congresses, and in the records of serious match play. We have the pleasure of laying before the student some novelties in the Opening that have been tested, and have excited much interest in the Chess circles of several large American cities.

$$1 \ \frac{\text{P-K4}}{\text{P-K4}} \qquad 2 \ \frac{\text{Kt-KB3}}{\text{Kt-QB3}} \qquad 3 \ \frac{\text{B-B4}}{\text{Kt-B3}}$$

Position after Black's 3rd move.

BLACK.

WHITE.

TWO KNIGHTS' DEFENCE.

(See Diagram on page 35.)

	1	2	3	4	5	6
	Vienna 1882 Congress.	London 1883 Congress.		New Orleans 1884.	New Orleans 1884.	New Orleans 1884.
	Bird Tschigorin	Bird Tschigorin		McConnell Zukertort	McConnell Zukertort	McConnell Zukertort
4	Kt-Kt5 / P-Q4			Kt-B3 (9) / B-Kt5 (10)		
5	PxP / Kt-QR4		B-KKt5 (7)	P-QR3 / BxKt		
6	B-Kt5ch / P-B3	P-Q3 (3) / P-KR3	KtxBP! / BxQ! (8)	QPxB / KtxP (11)		
7	PxP / PxP	Kt-KB3 / P-K5	KtxQ / Kt-QR4	BxPch / KxB		
8	B-K2 / P-KR3	Q-K2 / KtxB	KtxP! / KtxB	Q-Q5ch / K-Ksq		
9	Kt-KB3 / P-K5	PxKt / B-QB4	KxB / Kt-Kt5	QxKKt / P-Q4		
10	Kt-K5 / Q-B2	P-KR3 / Castles	K-K2 / R-QKtsq	Q-QR4 / Q-Q3	R-Bsq	
11	Kt-Kt4 (1) / BxKt	Kt-R2 / P-QKt4 (4)	P-Q3or / Kt3+	Castles / R-Bsq	Castles / RxKt (15)	KtxP? / Q-K2
12	BxB / B-Q3	Kt-QB3 / PxP		R-Ksq! / K-B2	PxR / B-R6	P-KB4 / B-Q2!
13	P-KR3 / CastlesKR	QxBP / Q-Q3		KtxPch! / KtxKt	R-Ksq / Q-B3	Castles / KtxKt
14	Kt-B3 / Kt-B5	Castles (5) / B-R3		B-B4 (12) / Kt-B6ch	Q-KB4! / K-Q2	Q-Q4 / Kt-B3
15	P-QKt3 / Kt-K4	Kt-Kt5 / Q-Kt3		PxKt / Q-KKt3ch	Q-Kt3 / B-B4	QxQP / B-K3
16	B-Kt2 (2) / KR-Ksq	P-QR4 / KtxP+ (6)		K-Rsq / Q-R4	B-Kt5 / Q-Kt3 (16)	Q-QKt5 / P-QR3
17	Castles / Kt(K4)xB			R-K3 / K-Ktsq	QR-Qsq / Q-B2	QxKtP / Q-B4ch
18	PxKt / Q-Q2			R-KKtsq / B-R6 (13)	R-Q2 / P-KR3	B-K3 / QxBch
19	Q-K2 / KtxP			Q-Q4 / Q-B2	B-K3 / R-Qsq	K-Rsq / Q-Kt3
20	P-Kt3 / Q-B4+			B-R6! / P-KKt3 (14)	P-Kt4 / K-Bsq 17)	QxQ / PxQ+

For Notes see page 38.

TWO KNIGHTS' DEFENCE.

(See Diagram on page 35.)

	4 Kt-Kt5 / P-Q4	5 PxP / Kt-QR4	6 B-Kt5ch / P-B3	7 PxP / PxP		8 B-K2 / P-KR3
	7	**8**	**9**	**10**	**11**	**12**
	Cincinnati, 1884. Zukertort Lukenbach	New York, 1879. Grundy Starbuck				
9	K-KB3 / B-Q3	P-K5				
10	P-Q3 / P-B4 (18)	Kt-K5 / Q-Q5				
11	Kt-B3 / Castles	P-KB4 / B-QB4				
12	Castles / P-R3	R-Bsq / Castles (22)				Q-Qsq (29)
13	B-K3 / B-Kt2 (19)	P-B3 / Q-Qsq				P-B3 / Kt-Q4
14	Kt-Q2 / Q-B2	P-QKt4 / Kt-Q4				P-QKt4 (30) / Q-R5ch
15	P-KB3 / P-K5	PxB / Q-R5ch	Q-B2 (24) / Q-R5ch		PxB? / Q-R5ch	P-Kt3 / QxRP
16	P-B4 / PxP	R-B2 / QxRP	P-Kt3 / QxRP	K-Qsq? / R-Qsq	P-Kt3 / QxRP	PxB / QxKtPch
17	BxP / KR-Ksq	P-Q4 / P-K6	QxKP / B-R6	P-Q4 (25) / PxP en pass	Q-R4 / QxKtPch	R-B2 / KtxKBP
18	R-Ksq (20) / BxBP!	R-B3 / Q-KtSch	PxB / BxR	BxP (26) / Kt-K6ch	K-Qsq (27) / R-Qsq	Q-R4 / Kt-R6
19	BxB / QxB	B-Bsq / P-B3	KxB / QxP	BxKt / BxB	K-B2 (28) / Q-Kt7	Kt-Kt4 / KtxR
20	Kt-Bsq / Q-Q5ch(21)	P-B4 / PxKt (23)	Q-B3+	PxKt / BxP+	QxKt / Kt-K6ch+	KtxKt / Q-B2+

NOTES, to pages 36 and 37.

(1) The previous moves are according to the most modern ideas in this Opening, but 11 P-KB4 is preferred for White.

(2) Lost time. B-K2 should have been played.

(3) Mr Bird think this move has merit, and deserves investigation.

(4) This move of Suhle's is generally thought to turn the game in favor of the second player.

(5) Bird's move, which Rev W Wayte pronounces much better than the "Handbuch's" Kt-R4.

(6) Mr Bird says he should have continued this game, 17 QxKt 17 P-QB3, 18 QxKP 18 PxKt, 19 P-R5 19 Q-B2, 20 B-B4, with a P more, and at least as good a position. But Mr Wayte does not think that Suhle's counter attack is thus proved a failure. The fault, he says, lies in Tschigorin's 15 Q-Kt3. The natural instinct of a strong player to keep White pinned as long as possible is here misleading. Black might have recovered the P, with at least an equal position, by two distinct modes of play: (A) 15 BxKt, 16 QxB 16 QxP, threatening to win the Q, and White's best reply is apparently 17 O-K2, since 17 P-QB4 would leave his Q awkwardly placed; (B) 15 QxP, 16 QxQ 16 KtxQ, 17 R-Qsq(c) 17 P-QB3!, 18 RxKt 18 PxR, 19 Kt-B7 19 B-Kt2, 20 KtxR 20 Rx Kt. (c) In this last variation 17 P-QB4 is inferior: 17 P-QB4 17 P-QB3, 18 PxKt 18 BxKt, 19 R-Qsq 19 QR-Qsq, and White must lose another P.

(7) This move was suggested by the Berlin "Schachzeitung." The analysis here is by S Euphrat and S A Charles, Cincinnati.

(8) If 6 Q-K2?, 7 P-QG 7 PxP, 8 P-KB3 8 B-R4, 9 KtxR 9 P-K5, 10 Castles 10 P-Q4, 11 B-K2 11 Q-B4ch, 12 K-Rsq, &c.+.

(9) This resolves the game into a variety of the Giuoco Piano, leading in this and the following two specimens to some very interesting play.

(10) The ordinary continuation here would be 4 B-B4, 5 P-Q3 5 P-Q3, 6 Kt-K2 or Castles, with an even game.

(11) A venturesome move.

(12) 14 Q-KB4ch is apparently better, e.g., 14 Q-KB4ch 14 K-K3 (if 14 K-Ktsq, 15 QxKt, remaining with a better game and a P ahead), 15 Q-KKt4ch, and if Black play 15 R-B4, 16 P-KB4.

(13) Intending QR-Ksq, but White's attack proves too vigorous.

(14) Continued 21 Q-R4! 21 B-K3, 22 BxR 22 RxB, 23 R(Ktsq)-Ksq 23 R-Ksq, 24 K-Ktsq! 24 B-Q2, 25 RxRch 25 BxR, 26 R-K7, and Black resigned.

(15) Mr Zukertort varies his play in this second trial, but his 11th move is probably overbold, and does not take into consideration White's effective 13th and 14th moves.

(16) Q-B2 at once appears better.

(17) Continued, 21 B-B5 (necessary to prevent Black from playing R-Q3 and thence to Kt3— White does well to sacrifice the B) 21 P-QKt3, 22 P-Kt5 22 Kt-R4, 23 B-Kt4 23 Kt-B5, 24 QR-K2 24 P-QR4, 25 PxP en pass 25 P-B4, 26 BxP 26 PxB, 27 R-Ktsq! 27 R-Q2, 28 RxP! 28 R-Q3, 29 P-R7 29 QxP, 30 RxB, and again White won.

(18) This move is a departure from the "Synopsis" (See page 44, Col. 7). The continuation there is 10 Castles, 11 P-B3 11 P-B4, 12 Castles 12 B-Kt2, 13 Q-R4 13 R-Bsq, and the variation is left without comment.

(19) Black has obtained the advantage in position, with all his forces well in hand to commence attacking operations.

(20) The P could not be saved.

(21) Continued, 21 K-Rsq 21 Kt-Kt5, and White resigns.

(22) This move, the invention of Mr Henry Loewe, Cincinnati, O., has proved to be one difficult to meet in actual play. As far as White's 12th move, the game is identical with Col. 5, page 43, of the "Synopsis" (see Diagram below), which proceeds, 12 Q-Q3 or B-Q3 for Black, and says it is doubtful if Black has an equivalent in position for the Pawn lost.

(23) Continued, 21 PxKt 21 PxBP, 22 BxP 22 PxB, 23 RxRch 23 KxR, 24 Q-B3ch 24 K-Ktsq, 25 Kt-B3 25 B-Kt5!, 26 Q-B4 26 R-KBsq, and Black wins.

(24) This move, or P-KKt3 is White's best resource.

(25) If 17 PxKt 17 Ktmates. If 17 QxKP 17 Kt-K6ch, and wins Q.

(26) If 18 KtxP 18 Kt-B5, 19 R-B3 19 B-Kt3+.

(27) R-B2 may be played.

(28) If 19 QxKt 19 Kt-K6mate.

(29) The late Mr D F M Starbuck, of Cincinnati, often played this novel variation with success. The usual move at this point is Q-Q3, followed by Kt-Kt2. The text move, however, leads to some fine situations.

(30) P-KKt3 is the only move.

PHILIDOR'S DEFENCE.

THE difficulty the second player experiences in this Opening in developing his game, is so well known that the Defence has been almost shelved. Hardly half a dozen noteworthy specimens of the " Philidor " have been going the rounds of the Chess columns during the last three years. The best estimate of the present standing of Philidor's Defence is contained in the following article, from a recent number of " Land and Water."

"The ' Philidor ' is a shrine of disappointment. Many analysts have worshipped thereat, and, rising from their knees with shining faces, have gone forth to announce that the secret had been confided to them. Their day of triumph has, however, been like the show of the Siberian sun in midwinter, sometimes glittering, but always very brief. The reason why such a deceptive oracle is so persistently consulted, lies in the yearnings of Chess players for some means whereby the detestable tyranny of the Ruy Lopez may be overthrown. The French Defence stands its ground, very much to the annoyance of first players, thus balked of their Ruy ; and if the ' Philidor ' could have but its legs made strong, second players would greatly rejoice, for no one likes the monotony of having but one defence. Apart from the lack of variety, there is a strain upon an exhaustion of the resources of a player, when thus bound down to a single Opening, as has often been manifested in the play of Blackburne, that faithful servant of the French Defence.

" The weakness of the ' Philidor ' consists in the fact of KPxQP being (apparently) incumbent on Black, whereby all his means of development become paralysed. Let us look at the board after 1 P-K4 1 P-K4, 2 Kt-KB3 2 P-Q3, 3 P-Q4 3 PxP, 4 QxP, and what do we see : White's Bishops have a free and unrestrained action, so have the Knights, and one of them is already in play He can quickly bring out what Pieces he pleases, and can Castle on either side as he likes. Being in possession of the Queen's file, he will naturally Castle on the Queen's side. Having done so, and all his Pieces being able to operate freely, either in combination or separately, he will have at his disposal an amount of power such as might seem sufficient to settle the issue right off.

" Very different is it with Black's unfortunate army. He can, it is true, play his QKt to B3, but that is an altogether illusory threat. His KB is hopelessly confined, and his QB has no good place to go to. His KKt has nothing particular in view when coming to B3, and, indeed, is itself often exposed to being attacked there ; while, as to the unhappy QP, it has obviously a most distressing future before it. Black's evil condition proceeds directly from 3 PxP. Could that capture be rendered unnecessary, his development, though slow, would be assured, and the future of the game would be such as skill, hand in hand with patience, might hopefully face.

" An end so desirable has attracted the attention of various analysts ; and particularly, Mr J Lord introduced 3 Kt-Q2. The defence, however, has not proved satisfactory, and, indeed, if met at once by 4 P-B3, as advised by Steinitz, we can see that it ought not to answer, considering that now White threatens B-QB4, followed by Q-Kt3. Our own opinion is, that unless Black can play 3 Kt-KB3, as recommended by Major Jaenisch, the ' Philidor ' is doomed. We are, however, by no means clear but that the move in question should stand. Let us set the moves. 1 P-K4 1 P-K4, 2 Kt-KB3 2 P-Q3, 3 P-Q4 3 Kt-KB3. White has three replies, namely 4 PxP, which is satisfactorily met by KtxP ; 4 B-KKt5, which Jaenisch answers with PxP ; and 4 Kt-B3, to which the Russian analyst again replies with PxP. As regards 4 B-KKt5, we will only say, respecting the capture of the Pawn, that we doubt its necessity, but it may pass for the present, as the inferiority which results is not very pronounced ; in respect, however, of 4 Kt-B3, which is the more dreaded line for White, we cannot but feel, first, that to capture the P must yield a bad game ; and secondly, that there is no necessity for such a continuation. As alternative, we suggest for Black, 4 QKt-Q2, continuing with P-KB3 if, and when necessary."

Since the above appeared, " Land and Water " has published the following further remarks on the Opening.—Ed. English Edition.

" Some time back we expressed an opinion that after 1 P-K4 1 P-K4, 2 Kt-KB3 2 P-Q3, 3 P-Q4, Black could advantageously continue with 3 Kt-KB3, having regard to certain improvements upon that continuation which we then suggested. It occurs to us now that we may as well support our hints with a few variations, and we proceed to do so. 3 P-Q4 3 Kt-KB3, 4 Kt-B3 (QKt-Q2, 5 B-QB4 5 B-K2, 6 Castles 6 P-B3, with a perfectly satisfactory game. Instead of 6 Castles, White could have played 6 Kt-KKt5, a highly interesting line, but as giving it here would distract the reader's attention, it is reserved as the wind up of this article. 3 P-Q4 3 Kt-KB3, 4 B-KKt5 4 QKt-Q2, 5 Kt-B3 5 P-B3, 6 BxKt 6 QxB, with a clear even game, to say no more, seeing that, as a matter of fact, we would take Black for choice. We may here remark that for a continuation in some natural lines subsequently, Black, discarding prejudices, may safely proceed with P-KKt3 and B-Kt2. We would further observe that in the 'Philidor,' as construed by us, KKt-B3, QKt-Q2, and P-B3 form a triangle, each of the angles depending on the other two.

"Having thus looked around, let us go on again: 3 P-Q4 3 Kt-KB3, 4 B-QB4 4 P-B3, 5 P-B3 5 B-K2, 6 Q-Kt3 6 Castles, with, of course, an even game; and indeed this variation is only given to show that 3 Kt-KB3 enables Black, in certain positions, to Castle early. 3 P-Q4 3 Kt-KB3, 4 PxP 4 KtxP, 5 B-QB4 5 P-QB3, 6 Castles 6 P-Q4, 7 B-Q3 7 Kt-B4, 8 B-K3 8 B-Kt5, and the game is equal. This a book variation. In lieu of 5 B-QB4, White might have played 5 B-Q3, but Black, by replying with Kt-B4, maintains a perfect equality. After 6 Castles, Black was not obliged to play P-Q4, as he had the option of playing B-K2, which move yields an even game. Having thus disposed of all specific lines that are evoked by 3 Kt-KB3, let us now look at the curious continuation to which we have previously referred. 3 P-Q4 3 Kt-KB3, 4 Kt-B3 4 QKt-Q2, 5 B-QB4 5 B-K2, 6 Kt-KKt5 6 Castles, 7 BxPch 7 RxB, 8 Kt-K6 8 Q-Ksq, 9 KtxBP 9 Q-Qsq, 10 KtxR.

Position after White's 10th move.

BLACK.

WHITE.

"It will easily be understood that the tenability of Black's game depends upon whether he can capture that presumptuous Knight, and it is also to be considered that Black is at present two Pawns behind, so that, if he has to pay but one other Pawn for that Knight, he will be, according to theory, numerically inferior. However, if the Knight can really be captured at the expense of another Pawn only, we, for our part, would be quite satisfied with Black's game, seeing that with his KR in possession of the KB file, and with his minor Pieces threatening to work in a powerful co-operation, there will be at his command all the materials of a strong attack. Our continuations will be as follow: 10 KtxR 10 P-QKt3, 11 Kt-Kt5 11 P-QR3, 12 QKt-B7 12 B-Kt2, and wins the Kt. If 12 KKt-B7 12 PxKt, 13 Kt-K6, and it will be seen that White could draw, in a very curious manner, by perpetually attacking the Queen. Black is certainly not called upon to struggle against such a result; but as many may feel, like us, disinclined to draw in such a position, we may point out that after 12 KKt-B7, Black can play Kt-Bsq, or Kt-Ktsq, and still win the Knight. In showing this we may as well return to White's tenth move, lest any student may have lost his grasp of the position. 10 KtxR 10 P-QKt3, 11 Kt-Kt5 11 P-QR3, 12 Kt(R8)-B7 12 Kt-Ktsq, 13 PxP 13 PxP, 14 QxQch 14 BxQ, 15 Kt-R7 (or Kt-Q6) 15 RxKt. Now for another variation: 10 KtxR 10 P-QKt3, 11 PxP 11 PxP, 12 Kt-Q5 12 KtxKt, 13 QxKt; Black may now play Kt-B3, a move that has far-reaching developments not unfavorable to him, or, in lieu thereof, continue with B-R3, 14 B-K3 14 Q-QBsq, 15 CastlesQR 15 Kt-B3, which wins the Kt at once, or B-B3, which saves the KP, and still allows of the Knight being won. There is also 13 B-R3, 14 Q-B6 14 Kt-Ktsq, 15 Q-B7 15 B-Kt2, winning the Knight, as White, if taking the QB, will lose his Queen. White might have played 15 Q-Q5, but Black, of course, still answers with B-Kt2.

"Another variation, and the last: 10 KtxR 10 P-QKt3, 11 PxP 11 PxP, 12 Kt-Kt5 12 P-QR3, 13 Kt-Q6 (13 QKt-B7 13 B-Kt2; or 13 KKt-B7 13 Kt-Ktsq, as in a previous variation) 13 BxKt, 14 QxB 14 B-Kt2, 15 Kt-B7 15 KtxP, 16 Kt-K6 16 Q-B3, and Black wins. Here we must conclude, and in doing so we may say, that though relying on 10 P-QKt3, as an answer to 10 KtxR, we do not consider that Black is absolutely confined to that particular move. It is indeed to be regretted that the simple lines of play whereby we hoped to improve the Philidor, should have such a complicated excrescence as 6 Kt-KKt5, but we rather fancy that when its effects are thoroughly mastered, 6 Kt-KKt5 will not be considered a good line for White to adopt."

PHILIDOR'S DEFENCE.

	1	2	3	4	5	6
	New Orleans, 1884.	Vienna 1882 Congress.	Coml Gaz Cor Tourney 1882.	Coml Gaz Cor Tourney 1882.		Living Chess Wakefield '83.
	McConnell Zukertort	Winawer Blackburne	Shaw Robertson	Narraway Robertson	Schulder Boden	J W Young E B Hussey
1	P-K4 / P-K4					
2	Kt-KB3 / P-Q3	Kt-QB3 (5) / Kt-KB3	Kt-KB3 / P-Q3			
3	B-B4 (1) / Kt-QB3 (2)	Kt-B3 / P-Q3	P-Q4 / PxP		P-B3 / P-KB4	P-Q4 / P-KB4
4	P-QR3 (3) / P-KB4	P-Q4 / PxP	KtxP / P-Q4	QxP / Kt-QB3	B-B4 / Kt-KB3	PxKP / BPxP
5	P-Q3 / Kt-B3	QxP / B-K2	PxP / QxP	B-QKt5 / B-Q2	P-Q4 / PxKP	Kt-Kt5 / P-Q4
6	B-KKt5 / P-KR3 (4)	B-KKt5 / Castles	Q-K2ch / B-K2	BxKt / BxB	PxP / PxKt	P-K6 / B-B4 (11)
7	BxKt / QxB	Castles / Kt-B3	Q-Kt5ch(7) / QxQ	B-Kt5 / Kt-B3	PxKt / QxP	Kt-QB3 (12 / P-B3
8	Kt-B3 / Kt-K2	Q-Q2 / B-K3	KtxQ / Kt-QR3	P-K5 (9) / PxP	PxP / Kt-B3	Kt-B7 / Q-B3
9	Kt-QKt5! / K-Qsq	P-QR3 / P-QR3	B-KB4 / P-QB3	QxPch / Q-K2	P-B4 / B-Q2	Q-Q2 / QBxP
10	Q-Q2 / P-B3	P-R3 / P-Kt4	Kt-Q6ch / BxKt	BxKt / PxB	B-K3 / Castles	KtxR / Kt-Q2
11	Kt-B3 / P-KKt4	BxKt / BxB	BxB / P-QKt3	QxQch / BxQ	Kt-Q2 / R-Ksq	Kt-R4 / P-K6
12	P-Q4 / PxQP	Kt-Q5 / BxKt	Kt-B3 / B-Kt2	QKt-Q2 / R-KKtsq	Q-B3 / B-B4	PxP / Q-R5ch
13	KtxQP / B-Kt2	PxB / Kt-K2	Castles / Castles	CastlesKR / Castles	CastlesQR / P-Q4	Q-B2 / QxKt
14	CastlesQR / PxP?	P-KKt3 / Kt-Kt3	P-KKt3 / Kt-B2	P-KKt3 / P-B4	BxP / QxPch	B-Q3 / Castles
15	Kt-K6ch! / BxKt	P-KR4 / R-Ksq	B-R3ch / K-Ktsq	QR-Qsq / B-B3	PxQ / B-R6mate.	BxP / KKt-B3
16	QxQPch / K-Ksq	P-R5 / Kt-K4	KR-Ksq / B-Bsq	P-Kt3 / B-B6		P-QKt3 / Q-KKt5
17	BxB / Kt-Q4	Kt-Q4 / P-Kt5!	BxKtch / KxB	P-KR4 / KR-Ksq		Kt-B7 / BxKt
18	Q-Q7ch / K-Bsq	QxP / R-Ktsq	RxR / KxR	P-R4 / R-K7		B-B5 / B-Kt5ch
19	BxKt / R-Qsq	Q-R4 / Kt-B6!	BxB / KxB	Kt-Ktsq / RxR		B-Q2 / BxBch
20	QxKtP+	Kt-Kt3 / Q-K2 (6)	R-K8ch / K-Q2 (8)	RxR / BxKt (10)		KxB / Kt-K5ch (13

For Notes see page 42.

F

NOTES, to page 41.

(1) A continuation favored by Mr Boden, but generally held to be inferior to 3 P-Q4. Of late, however, several strong players, including Mr Blackburne, have given the text move some attention.

(2) Harrwitz's move, B-K2, is more usual, and apparently stronger.

(3) To provide a retreat for the B, should the adverse Kt attack from R4, but P-Q4 is preferable.

(4) Again B-K2 would be better.

(5) The game becomes substantially a Philidor in a few moves.

(6) Continued 21 R-Q3 21 R-Kt3, 22 P-B3 22 KR-Ktsq, 23 B-B2 23 Q-K7, 24 KR-Bsq 24 B-Kt4ch, 25 K-Ktsq 25 Kt-Q7ch, 26 RxKt 26 BxR, 27 R-Qsq 27 RxKt!, 28 BxR 28 BxP, 29 B-B2 (if PxB then QxRch) 29 RxPch, 30 K-Bsq 30 R-Ktsq, 31 Q-K4 31 R-Kt8ch!, 32 KxR 32 Q-Kt4ch, 33 Q-Kt4 33 Bx Q, and Black wins.

(7) The "Synopsis" (page 21, col 5) proceeds here 7 Kt-Kt5 7 Kt-QR3, 8 QKt-B3 8 Q-Qsq, &c., leading to an even game.

(8) As these contestants are experienced and skillful correspondence players, we give the remaining moves: 21 R-R8 21 K-K3, 22 Kt-K2 22 P-QB4, 23 P-QB4 23 P-Kt3, 24 RxP 24 Kt-B3, 25 Kt-B4ch 25 K-Q3, 26 RxP 26 Kt-Q2, 27 P-QR4 27 P-KKt4, 28 Kt-Q5 28 K-B3, 29 K-Q2 29 P-R4, 30 P-R3 30 R-R3, 31 R-B5 31 P-Kt5, 32 P-R4 32 K-Q3, 33 Kt-B4 33 Kt-B3, 34 K-K3 34 K-B3, 35 R-Kt5 35 R-Rsq, 36 R-Kt6 36 R-Ksqch, 37 K-Q3 37 R-Qsqch, 38 Kt-Q5, and White wins.

(9) Not in the books. The approved continuation is 8 Kt-B3 8 B-K2, 9 CastlesQR 9 Castles, 10 KR-Ksq 10 Kt-Q2, even game.

(10) Continued 21 P-KKt4 21 RxQBP, and White resigns.

(11) Kt-KR3 is the usual move.

(12) It would be better to play 7 KtxKP 7 PxKt, 8 Q-R5ch ; but games played at exhibitions of "Living Chess" are not a fair subject for critical notes.

(13) Continued 21 BxKt 21 PxB, 22 KR-KBsq 22 P-KKt3, 23 K-B3 23 Kt-K4, 24 P-KR3 24 Q-K3, 25 Q-R4 25 Q-Q4, 26 K-Kt2 26 Q-B4, 27 QR-Qsq 27 Q-R4, 28 QxP 28 Kt-B5ch, 29 PxKt, and Black drew by perpetual check.

FOUR KNIGHTS' GAME AND THREE KNIGHTS' GAME.

THE Four Knights' Game has scarcely a history outside of the tournaments and matches of the last six years. It is a conservative Opening, leading to a free exchange of minor Pieces at an early stage, and to a slow, cautious middle Game. It avoids a speedy, direct attack with a small force, and brings the Knights and Bishops forward, as if to get rid of some of them without advantage on either side would facilitate matters. The admirers of the Opening, for off-hand play, are very few.

———

THE Three Knights' Game is less of a "trading-off" debut, and often quickly runs into fine combinations, resembling, however, those of better known Openings. Its individuality is slight; and its recorded analysis, in English, at least, is brief.

———

$$1 \; \frac{\text{P-K4}}{\text{P-K4}} \qquad 2 \; \frac{\text{Kt-KB3}}{\text{Kt-QB3}} \qquad 3 \; \frac{\text{Kt-B3}}{}$$

Position after White's 3rd move.

BLACK.

WHITE.

For 3 Kt-B3, see cols 1-4; for 3 P-KKt3, see col 5; and for 3 B-B4, see col 6; on next page.

	1	2	3	4	5	6
	FOUR KNIGHTS' GAME.				**THREE KNIGHTS' GAME.**	
	Vienna 1882 Congress.	London 1883 Congress.	New Orleans 1884.	3rd French Nat Tour '83.	London 1883 Congress.	London 1883 Congress.
	Schwarz Mackenzie	Englisch Rosenthal	Steinitz Buck Dunn &c.	Clerc De Rivière	Blackburne Steinitz	Steinitz Bird
1	P-K4 P-K4				P-K4 P-K4	
2	Kt-KB3 Kt-QB3				Kt-KB3 Kt-QB3	
3	Kt-B3 Kt-B3				P-KKt3	B-B4 (15)
4	B-Kt5 B-B4	B-Kt5 (6)		P-QR3 (12)	P-Q4 PxP	KtxP KtxKt
5	Castles P-Q3 (1)	Castles Castles		BxKt QPxB	KtxP B-Kt2	P-Q4 B-Q3
6	P-Q4 PxP	P-Q3 P-Q3	Kt-Q5 KtxKt	KtxP KtxP	B-K3 Kt-B3	PxKt BxP
7	KtxP B-Q2	B-Kt5 BxKt	PxKt Kt-K2	KtxKt Q-Q5	B-K2 Castles	B-Q3 Kt-K2
8	KtxKt PxKt	PxB P-KR3 (7)	P-B3 (10) B-R4	Castles QxKKt	Castles Kt-K2	Castles P-QB3
9	B-Q3 Castles	B-KR4 B-Kt5 (8)	P-Q6 PxP	R-Ksq B-K3	B-B3 P-Q3	Q-R5 P-Q3 !
10	Kt-R4 B-Kt3	P-KR3 B-Q2 (9)	P-Q4 P-K5	P-Q4 Q-Q4	Q-Q2 Kt-Q2	P-B4 B-Q5ch
11	KtxB RPxKt	R-Ktsq P-QKt3 ?	Kt-Kt5 P-Q4	Kt-B3 Q-Q2	B-R6 Kt-K4	K-Rsq P-KKt3
12	P-KB4 Q-K2	P-Q4 R-Ksq	B-R4 P-Q3	B-Kt5 P-R3	BxB KxB	Q-K2 K-Q2 ?
13	R-Ksq (2) P-Q4	R-Ksq P-Kt4 ?	Q-R5 B-B4	Q-R5 P-KKt3	B-K2 P-KB3	B-B4 P-KB4
14	PxP Q-B4ch	KtxKtP ! PxKt	B-Kt3 B-KKt3	Q-R4 B-Kt2	P-B4 Kt-B2	R-Qsq BxKt (16)
15	B-K3 QxQP	BxP PxP ?	Q-K2 P-KR3	B-K3 P-KKt4	QR-Qsq P-B3	PxB PxP
16	P-B4 Q-Q3	PxP R-K4 ?	Kt-R3 P-B4	Q-Kt3 CastlesQR	B-B4 B-Q2	B-R3 P-Q4
17	P-KR3 (3) P-B4	PxR QKtxP	Kt-B4 B-B2	QR-Qsq P-KB4	BxKt RxB	QxP P-QKt4
18	Q-B2 KR-Ksq	P-KB4 Kt-Kt3	P-KR4 Q-Q2	P-B4 B-B3	P-B5 Kt-Bsq	BxKtP PxB
19	QR-Qsq (4) Q-B3	BxB QxB	P-R5 K-R2	B-B2 Q-Q3	P-K5 ! BPxP	BxKt K-B3 (17)
20	P-QKt3 QR-Qsq (5)	BxKt+	Q-K3 B-Qsq (11)	Q-K3 KR-Ksq (13)	Kt-K6ch BxKt (14)	Q-K5 Q-Q2 (18)

For Notes see page 45.

NOTES, to page 44.

(1) Mr Sellman recalls the fact that, in the First American Chess Congress (1857), Morphy at this point played Castles, and won; and remarks that the termination was of such remarkable depth and brilliancy, as to rank it among the immortal games.

(2) White has made a skillful Opening.

(3) Tame. Mr Ranken suggests as better, 17 P-B5 17 PxP, 18 Q-B2, followed next move by QR-Qsq.

(4) Threatening BxRPch.

(5) Continued, 21 B-B2 21 RxRch, 22 BxR 22 R-Ksq, 23 B-B3 23 P-Kt3, 24 B-Kt2 24 B-Bsq, 25 Q-B3 25 K-Kt2 (inferior to R-K3), 26 B-KBsq 26 Q-K3, 27 P-KKt4 27 B-Kt2, 28 P-Kt5 28 K-Bsq, 29 Px Kt 29 Q-K5, 30 Q-Kt3 30 Q-B7, 31 R-Ksq! (if Black captures the B he loses his Q) 31 R-K5, 32 RxR 32 QxR, 33 B-K5 33 P-R4, 34 K-B2 34 Q-B7ch, 35 B-K2, and Black resigned.

(6) This game was the last played in the Congress, and resulted in Englisch tieing with Mackenzie and Mason for fifth, sixth, and seventh prizes.

(7) Mr Steinitz says this is weak. He prefers 8 Kt-K2, a move that cannot be made after the KRP is moved.

(8) Lost time. He should play B-Q2 at once.

(9) The same authority prefers here 10 BxKt, and 11 P-Kt4.

(10) The usual continuation is 8 KtxP 8 KtxP, 9 P-QB3, and White is thought to have slightly the better game.

(11) Continued, 21 Q-R3 21 P-R4, 22 P-R4 22 R-Bsq, 23 B-Qsq 23 R-B2, 24 R-R3 24 R-QB3, 25 B-K2 25 R-Kt3, 26 B-Kt5 26 Q-Bsq, 27 P-QKt3 27 Kt-Ktsq, 28 P-B4 (Mr Steinitz pronounced this advance premature, and held that 28 B-Q2 would have given him a decided advantage) 28 B-Kt4. Black won on the 80th move, after a seven hours' contest, in three sittings.

(12) M Rosenthal says the best move here is B-Kt5.

(13) Continued, 21 Q-R3 21 B-Kt2 (M Rosenthal believes Black could have won by 21 QxBP), 22 Q-R5 22 R-Ktsq, 23 Q-Kt6 23 B-Q2 (M Rosenthal says that this move gives White the better game), 24 QxQ 24 PxQ, 25 B-Kt3 25 B-Bsq, 26 P-Q5? This weak move permitted the Black KB to enter the game. Black won on the 46th move.

(14) Continued, 21 PxB 21 R-K2, 22 Q-Kt5 22 Q-Ksq, 23 R-Q3 23 RxP?, 24 R-R3 24 Q-K2, and White mated in three moves.

(15) Dr Zukertort says this is an inferior defence. He would bring out the other Kt, running into the Four Knights' Game.

(16) If B-Kt3 White wins by P-K5.

(17) If QxB White would continue 20 RxPch 20 K-Ksq, 21 R-K5+.

(18) Continued, 21 QxR 21 QxB, 22 R-Ksq 22 Q-Q3, 23 R-K8 23 Q-Q2, 24 QR-Ksq 24 Q-QB2, 25 Q-B6ch 25 K-B4, 26 QR-K6 26 BxR, 27 RxB, and Black resigned.

THE QUEEN'S BISHOP'S PAWN GAME.

THIS Opening is also known as "Staunton's Opening," and the "English Knight's Opening." The "Synopsis" says, without qualification, that full analysis has shown that it is not to be recommended for the first player. Chess periodicals may be examined for months, without finding a specimen of it. Mr Staunton said of it, in 1848, that "it deserves, and if we mistake not will yet attain, a higher place in the category of legitimate Openings than has hitherto been assigned to it." Twenty-five years later he wrote that the Opening had been grudgingly admitted into favor, and that another quarter of a century would possibly be required to enable it "to take the rank it deserves among our best debut." This opinion has not been verified, and there are but slight indications that it will be.

Mr W N Potter has recently written two brief articles on the Opening, in which he takes, if not a favorable, at least a neutral position regarding its merits. He says:

"As to some defences, we fancy the last words have yet to be said. Take, for instance, Steinitz's Defence : 1 P-K4 1 P-K4, 2 Kt-KB3 2 Kt-QB3, 3 P-B3 3 P-Q4 1, 4 Q-R4 4 P-B3. This last move was adopted by Steinitz against Wisker in 1868, and ever since its introduction on that occasion has been highly esteemed. Zukertort thought so well of 4 P-B3 that he adopted it against Rosenthal in their match. Wisker and Rosenthal both continued with 5 B-Kt5 ; and Steinitz and Zukertort both replied with KKt-K2. Wisker then continued with 6 PxP, getting thereby a bad game. Rosenthal's continuation was 6 P-Q3, and Zukertort answered with B-Q2, whereupon followed 7 PxP 7 KtxP, and Black has undoubtedly the better game. Now, according to our opinion, Rosenthal's sixth move was all right, but his seventh was a material aid to Black in developing. Let the moves be replayed : 1 P-K4 1 P-K4, 2 Kt-KB3 2 Kt-QB3, 3 P-B3 3 P-Q4, 4 Q-R4 4 P-B3, 5 B-Kt5 5 KKt-K2, 6 P-Q3 6 B-Q2. We now play for White, 7 Q-B2, and are unable to perceive that Black has the slightest superiority. This, by way of a first step, and because we do not want to inflict too violent a shock upon those who assume that 4 Q-R4, met by P-B3, subjects White to a crushing disadvantage.

"It is a pity that the spirit of originality does not more obtain amongst analysts and players, instead of so much following of the bell. Well, there is 7 Q-B2, by which move White means to keep the position as it is, quietly developed, and leave Black to unlock himself. The following is a probable variation, and it is one which we believe will be accepted with but slight modifications, as containing the best line of play on both sides : 7 Q-B2 7 P-QR3, 8 B-R4 8 P-QKt4, 9 B-Kt3 9 B-Kt, 10 Castles (B-K3 has its claims, but it impedes the development of the QKt) 10 Q-Q2, or Q3, and the game seems to us about equal. Black's position is stronger in some respects, but he is subjected to counter-balancing disadvantages. Should he intend to Castle on the King's side, there will be loss of time, and also a weakening of his strong points. Should he Castle on the Queen's side, he must prepare for a very formidable attack, and, indeed, such an operation seems out of the question, if theoretical doctrines and practical lessons stand for anything. There are divers modifications, after arriving at White's tenth move, that are worth pointing out : 10 Castles 10 Q-Q2, 11 B-K3 11 Kt-Kt3, 12 R-Qsq, and White's game is good, as he now threatens P-Q4, with effect, and, moreover, he now proposes to release QKt, seeing that, as the position stands, it can go to Q2, and thence to KBsq. The idea that the QKt could not go to Q2, on account of P-Q5, will be dispelled, if the student only looks two moves before him. Black, to prevent the QKt thus coming out, may bring his QR on to the scene. As to this, we go back to White's tenth move—10 Castles 10 Q-Q2, 11 B-K3 11 Kt-Kt3, 12 R-Qsq 12 R-Qsq. Here White may play 13 P-Q4, which promises more than it can perform, but which, nevertheless, performs quite enough for equality, or he may simplify by 13 PxP 13 BxP, 14 QKt-Q2, where we leave him fully developed, and subject to no inferiority of position."

Mr J Reichhelm, of Philadelphia, does not agree with Mr Potter as to White's ability to make an effective answer to Black's 4 P-B3, which Mr Reichhelm terms "a crushing rejoinder." He says :

"Remember, it is part of Steinitz's system of play that, when the adverse King's Bishop is either off the board, or not in a situation to effectively play to QB4, then the King's Pawn is best defended by Pawn at B3. This hinders all attacks of Kt, or B-KKt5, and, in a great measure, bottles up the attack."

Mr Potter, in "Land and Water," proposes that the first player should continue thus, his innovation resting on White's seventh move :

"5 B-Kt5 5 Kt-K2, 6 P-Q3 6 B-Q2, 7 Q-B2, and White is under no disadvantage. Even assuming this to be absolutely correct, if the first player is compelled to battle to barely hold his own in the position so early as the seventh move, this Opening may be quietly laid away on the shelf."

Resuming the subject in the second article, Mr Potter remarks that he does not allege that "Staunton's Opening" is a particularly good method of commencing, but his position is, that the maledictions heaped upon it by analysts are, in his opinion, undeserved. He says:

"We lately gave our reasons for supposing that (the line of play given above) yields no such game as White should fear, and we rather fancy the same may be said of the forms of 3 P-Q4. At any rate they, with 3 P-B4, may wait until there is more demand for an examination of their claims than at present exists. The most formidable enemy of the "Staunton Attack" is 3 Kt-B3. The recognised reply is 4 P-Q4, with KtxKP or P-Q4 as Black's rejoinder. Here Mr Edward Marks steps in and proposes PxP, as another fourth move that Black can adopt. He sends us an analysis, wherefrom we extract the following lines (beginning each time at White's third move) 3 P-B3 3 Kt-B3, 4 P-Q4 4 PxP, 5 PxP 5 B-Kt5ch, with the better game; 3 P-B3 3 Kt-B3, 4 P-Q4 4 PxP, 5 PxP 5 KtxP, and again Black for choice; 3 P-B3 3 Kt-B3, 4 P-Q4 4 PxP, 5 B-KKt5 5 PxP, and such attack as White may have, will scarcely compensate him for being a Pawn behind; 3 P-B3 3 Kt-B3, 4 P-Q4 4 PxP, 5 P-K5, Black has three replies, namely, 5 Kt-Q4, 5 Kt-K5, and 5 Q-K2. Mr Marks sends us variations upon each, but they open up issues that cannot be satisfactorily dealt with in the limits at our disposal. We may, however, mention, as one of the main points, that Black threatens to break up White's centre, by P-Q3, on which account Mr Steinitz, to whom Mr Marks submitted his variations, condemned White's game, as a whole.

"Our own examination of 4 P-Q4 4 PxP, has not had the effect of making us perfectly assured of the goodness of Mr Marks' defence; but that question becomes of minor importance in our eyes, on account of the general feeling we have against P-Q4 itself. We prefer either 4 Q-R4, or 4 B-Kt5. The former, if we mistake not, is now suggested for the first time; while as to the latter, though not new, it has been hitherto wrongly continued. We will take them in succession: 4 Q-R4 4 B-K2, 5 B-Kt5, with the better game; 4 Q-R4 4 P-Q4, 5 KtxP, and White for choice; 4 Q-R4 4 P-QR3, 5 B-B4 (if 5 B-Kt5, then KtxP, and Black appears to us to obtain the superiority, though on this point we would be gladly convicted of error, whereas PxB we do not fear) 5 P-Q4, 6 PxP 6 KtxP, 7 KtxP 7 Q-K2, 8 BxKt 8 QxKtch, 9 Q-K4, and White is a Pawn ahead, with no disadvantage in position. Had Black played 7 P-QKt4, then 8 KtxKt, to say nothing of 8 BxKtP, which could, however, have been profitably played. As far as we can see, 4 Q-R4 can stand. It is obvious that 4 P-QR3, 5 B-B4 5 KtxP, 6 BxPch 6 KxB, 7 QxKt, produces no inferiority for White, to say no more; and therefore, after 4 Q-R4 4 P-QR3, 5 B-B4, Black appears to have nothing better than B-K2 or B-B4. Either of these moves is doubtless good enough for equality, but Black ought to aim at something more than an even game, if the unfavourable opinions of various analysts are to be maintained. It is true that, after 4 Q-R4, Black can play at once B-B4; but then 5 B-Kt5, and White has rather the better game.

"As to the other line mentioned, namely, 4 B-Kt5, the usual continuation is 4 KtxP, 5 Castles, but we would play 5 Q-K2 5 Kt-Q3, 6 KtxP, and if White suffer from any inequality, we should like it to be made known to us."

We conclude this debate on a neglected Opening with a game, at this debut, played in July 1883, at the Nuremburg Congress, with notes from "The Field"

WHITE.	BLACK.
Mr Winawer.	Mr Riemann.

1 P-K4	1 P-K4	
2 Kt-KB3	2 Kt-QB3	
3 P-B3	3 P-Q4	
4 Q-R4	4 PxP	(1)
5 KtxP	5 Q-Q4	
6 KtxKt	6 PxKt	
7 P-Q4	7 PxP en pass	
8 BxP	8 QxB	(2)
9 QxPch	9 K-Qsq	
10 QxR	10 B-Q3	
11 B-K3 (3)	11 Kt-B3	
12 Kt-Q2 (4)	12 Kt-Q4	
13 P-KR4	13 K-K2	(5)
14 QxP	14 B-KKt5	
15 Kt-B3	15 KtxP	
16 PxKt	16 QxPch	
17 K-K2	17 Q-B5ch	
18 K-Qsq	18 BxKtch	
19 PxB	19 Q-Q4ch	
20 B-Q2	20 QxPch	
21 K-B2	21 Q-K5ch	
22 K-Kt3	22 Q-Q4ch	
23 K-B2	23 Q-K5ch	

Drawn Game.

(1) Inferior 4 P-B3 is the proper continuation.

(2) This capture is unsound, and ought to involve the loss of the game, if properly followed up by Black.

(3) If White had played now 11 Q-B3, Black's game would have been irretrievably lost. Winawer remarked that he knew the move well enough, and played this variation on the strength of it; but somehow, at the last moment, changed his mind.

(4) Now it is too late to retire Q to B3, because of 12 B-KKt5, &c.

(5) 13 R-Ksq would have been more forcible, and probably have won the game. If, in answer, White Castles, Black wins with 14 KtxP, &c.

THE QUEEN'S PAWN COUNTER GAMBIT. THE HUNGARIAN DEFENCE.

THESE Openings are not brought near together because they have any resemblance; indeed, they are antithetical. In the Queen's Pawn Counter Gambit Black at once tries to seize the attack. In the Hungarian Defence the second player takes a very quiet line of play, looking to a safe and substantial development of his game, before either sustaining or attempting a serious attack. The Queen's Pawn Counter Game does not stand high in the esteem of analysts. The Hungarian Defence has not received much attention from them, the debut being so conservative that, like a fortunate people, it has but little history. It enables Black to avoid the Evans and kindred attacks, and it is believed to be sound in all respects. The fact that it is not mentioned by Staunton, Bird, Wormald, Gossip, or Cook is due to its not having attracted much notice from players and analysts. The reputation it has is fair.

QUEEN'S PAWN COUNTER GAMBIT.

	1. P-K4 / P-K4	2. Kt-KB3 / P-Q4	3. PxP / QxP	4. Kt-B3 / Q-R4	5. B-B4 / Kt-QB3
	1	2	3	4	5
6	Castles / B-KKt5 (1)	P-Q3 (3) / B-QKt5	B-K3		
7	BxPch (2) / KxB	B-Q2 / Kt-B3!	BxB / PxB		
8	Kt-Kt5ch / Kmoves	P-QR3 / BxKt	Castles / Castles		
9	QxB+	BxB / Q-B4	R-Ksq / B-Q3	P-KR3	
10		Castles / B-Kt5 (4)	Kt-Kt5+	P-QR3 / B-Q3	Q-B4 / P-QKt4
11		P-Kt4+ (5)		B-Q2 / Kt-B3	Q-Q3
12				P-QKt4+	B-Kt2+

(1) We are indebted to Mr George Tatnall, Wilmington, Del., for the analysis on this page.

(2) It is strange that this move has been overlooked. Mr Staunton and others even proceed a few moves, and give Black an even game.

(3) After diligent analysis, Mr Tatnall regards this move as very strong. He says it wins a P for White, or gives him a great superiority in position.

(4) He dare not Castle.

(5) These were the opening moves in a game in "The Commercial Gazette" Correspondence Tourney, between Mr Tatnall and Mr J W Shaw, Montreal, Canada. White obtained the advantage in the Opening, but through some minor errors did not win until the 80th move.

HUNGARIAN DEFENCE.

1. $\dfrac{\text{P-K4}}{\text{P-K4}}$ 2. $\dfrac{\text{Kt-KB3}}{\text{Kt-QB3}}$ 3. $\dfrac{\text{B-B4}}{\text{B-K2}}$ 4. P-Q4

	1	2	3	4	5	6
4	P-Q3					PxP
5	Castles / Kt-B3	PxP / PxP (2)	P-Q5 — / Kt-Kt1—(3	P-B3 (4) / Kt-B3	P-B4	Castles / Kt-B3
6	P-Q5 / Kt-QKtsq	QxQ— / BxQ—		Q-B2 / Castles (5)	Q-Kt3 / Kt-R4 (6)	R-Ksq / Castles
7	Kt-B3 / Castles (1)			B-K2 / B-Kt5	Q-R4ch / P-B3	P-K5 / Kt-Ksq
8				B-K3—	BxKt / RxKt	KtxP / P-Q4
9					PxKP+	KtxKt / PxKt
10						B-Q3 / P-Kt3 (7)

(1) Mr Potter considers that Black has an excellent game. Black now proposes to play Kt-Ksq, followed by P-KB4, with a probability, unless met with nice play, of obtaining a superiority in position. In playing 3 B-K2 Mr Potter says that Black supports his Q at the very moment she wants support.

(2) KtxP will not do, e.g.: 5 KtxP, 6 KtxKt 6 PxKt, 7 Q-R5+.

(3) White's move, 5 P-Q5, has the effect of depriving White of the slight advantage properly belonging to the first move. Mr Potter remarks that extended analysis of the Hungarian is not required, simplicity being its special characteristic. The " Handbuch's " suggested variation at this point is 5 P-Q5 5 Kt-Ktsq, 6 B-Q3 6 B-Kt5, 7 Castles 7 Kt-KB3, 8 P-B4 8 P-B3, 9 Kt-B3 9 Kt-R3.

(4) This, and the following column, are from the German "Handbuch." 5 P-B3 seems to be a better move for White than those suggested by Mr Potter.

(5) If 6 B-Kt5, 7 B-QKt5. If 6 PxP, 7 PxP 7 P-Q4, 8 PxP 8 KtxP, 9 B-Kt5+.

(6) If 6 Kt-B3, 7 Kt-Kt5 7 Kt-QR4, 8 Q-R4ch 8 P-B3, 9 B-K6+.

(7) Continued, 11 Kt-Q2 11 Kt-Kt2, 12 Kt-B3 12 P-B3 (premature, since it affords White the opportunity for commencing an immediate attack), 13 Kt-Q4 (best; this, as will be seen anon, obtains a decided advantage in position. Black has already a very difficult game to play) 13 PxP, 14 KtxP 14 Q-Q3, 15 KtxKP 15 B-R5 (B-B3 is better), 16 P-KKt3 16 P-B3, 17 B-KB4 17 P-Kt4, 18 Kt-B7 18 Q-Kt3, 19 KtxP 19 BxKt, 20 BxB 20 QxBPch, 21 K-Rsq 21 B-R6 (B-Kt2 would be still better), 22 B-KBsq 22 BxB, 23 RxB 23 Q-QB4, 24 B-B4 24 QR-Ksq, 25 Q-Q2 25 Kt-K3, 26 B-R6 26 RxRch, 27 RxR 27 Q-B5, 28 Q-Ksq 28 Kt-Bsq, and White announced mate in five moves.

THE VIENNA GAME.

THE Vienna Game, with its ramifications, is the subject of much interest in the Chess World, and some important discoveries have been made in it within a year or two.

NOTES, to opposite page.

(1) P-Q4 is the usual move.

(2) B-Q2 was the proper move.

(3) M Rosenthal, from whose notes to this game we quote, does not approve of this move. He regards it as losing time. White should play 3 B-B4, or 3 Kt-B3.

(4) Black should have played here B-B4, followed by P-Q3, a position identical with one in the Ruy Lopez.

(5) The proper play, 4 B-Kt5, 5 Kt-Q5 5 KtxKt, or B-K2.

(6) B-B4 is better.

(7) B-B4, followed by Castles, is preferable.

(8) This attack on the Q side is premature, the Pawns on this side being weakened for the end game.

(9) Weak. P-Q4 should have been played.

(10) A premature attack.

(11) M Rosenthal would have preferred 20 Kt-K2 20 CasKR!, 21 BxKt 21 PxB, 22 Q-B2, followed by Kt-Kt3+. The game was equal at the 38th move; but, through Black's weak play at that point. White won on the 58th move.

(12) Lost time. He should have played at once 9 P-KB4 9 PxP, 10 KtxP, because now BxKtP is not to be feared.

(13) B-Q5 would have been fatal.

(14) In seeking to avoid the exchange of Queens, Mr Steinitz did not observe that his Q had no good square to go to. M Rosenthal says he should have played 14 Kt-B3, 15 Q-Bsq, and then retreat.

(15) This mistake should have lost the game. He should have accepted the exchange of Queens, then played Kt-K2, remaining with a good game.

(16) Too hasty with the attack. B-K3 would have won easily.

(17) If R moves, Black makes the paralyzing reply, P-Kt5.

(18) The usual attack is Kt-Q5.

(19) M Rosenthal, in a general way, dislikes this move. It opens the way for a combination in which an adversary can sacrifice his QB.

(20) Lost time. Kt-K2 was the move.

(21) Again lost time.

(22) Weak. White should have kept his B, to take part in a counter attack.

(23) Continued, 21 Kt-R6 21 R-Kt2, 22 KR-Ktsq 22 R-QKtsq, 23 P-R5 23 Q-Bsq, 24 P-Kt3 24 Kt-K2, 25 P-R4 25 PxP, a weak move. Black could have won a Pawn and the game at this point, by P-Kt5. After a protracted struggle, Black won.

(24) 21 PxR 21 RxP, and White resigns. One of twelve simultaneous games played by Dr Zukertort.

VIENNA OPENING.

	1	2	3	4	5	6
	Vienna 1882 Congress.	St. Louis, 1884.	Match 1881 Paris.	Paris, 1882. Clerc and De Rivière v	2nd French Nat Tour '81.	Cincinnati, 1884.
	Schwarz Winawer	Zukertort Max Judd	Clerc De Rivière	Steinitz	Clerc Chamier	Zukertort Ettlinger
1	P-K4 / P-K4					
2	Kt-QB3 / B-B4		— / Kt-QB3			
3	Kt-B3 / P-Q3	P-B4 / P-Q3	B-Kt5 (3) / Kt-B3 (4)	— / P-QR3	Kt-B3 / Kt-B3	
4	Kt-QR4 / B-Kt3	Kt-B3 / Kt-KB3	Kt-B3 / Kt-Q5 (5)	B-R4 / P-KKt3	B-Kt5 / B-Kt5	— / P-Q3
5	KtxB / RPxKt	B-B4 / Castles	B-R4 (6) / KtxKtch	Kt-B3 / B-Kt2	Castles (18) / Castles	P-Q4 / B-Q2
6	B-B4 (1) / B-Kt5	P-Q3 / P-B3	QxKt / P-B3 (7)	P-Q3 / Kt-Q5	P-Q3 / P-Q3	Castles / P-KR3
7	P-KR3 / B-R4	PxP / PxP	P-Q3 / P-QR4 (8)	Kt-K2 / KtxKKtch	P-KR3 (19) / Kt-K2	BxKt / BxB
8	P-Q3 / P-R3	Kt-K2 / Q-K2	P-QR3 / P-QKt4	PxKt / Q-R5	B-Kt5 / P-B3	PxP / KtxP
9	P-KKt4 / B-Kt3	Kt-Kt3 / P-QKt4	B-Kt3 / P-Q3	P-B3 (12) / Q-R6	B-QB4 / K-Rsq!	PxP / QxP
10	R-KKtsq / P-QB3	B-Kt3 / Kt-R3	Castles / P-R3	P-KB4 / Q-Kt7	Kt-KR4(20) / KKt-Ktsq	Q-K2 / P-B4
11	Q-K2 / Kt-Q2	Q-K2 / K-Rsq	Q-Kt3 / P-Kt4	Kt-Kt3 / P-KR4	Q-R5 (21) / P-KKt3	Kt-Q2 / Castles
12	P-R3 / P-Kt4	Kt-R4 (2) / B-KKt5	B-K3 / Q-K2	P-R4 / P-QKt4	Q-K2 / P-B3	QKtxKt / PxKt
13	B-R2 / Kt-Kt3	Q-Bsq / KtxP	P-B3 (9) / B-KKt2	B-Kt3 / P-Q3	B-Q2 / P-KKt4	KtxP / Q-Kt3
14	B-K3 / P-QB4	Kt(R4)-B5 / Q-Qsq	Q-B2 / B-R3	Q-K2! (13) / PxP (14)	Kt-B3 / Kt-Kt3	Kt-Kt3 / P-KR4
15	P-B3 / Q-K2	B-R6 / B-B7ch	P-KR4 (10) / Kt-Q2	BxP / B-Kt5	Kt-R2 / BxKt	P-KB3 / B-B4ch
16	P-KR4 / B-R2	QxB / KtxQ	Q-Kt3 / B-B3	Q-Bsq / Q-B6 (15)	PxB / Q-K2	K-Rsq / P-R5
17	P-Kt5 / P-R4	BxPch / K-Ktsq	P-R5 / Kt-B4	B-Kt5 / P-KB3	P-QR4 / Q-Kt2	Kt-K4 / KR-Ksq
18	Kt-Q2 / B-Kt3	KxKt / R-Ksq	B-R2 / P-QKt5	B-Qsq (16) / PxB	Q-R5 / B-Q2	B-B4 / P-R6
19	Kt-Bsq / Q-B2	B-R6 / BxKt	PxP / PxP	BxQ / BxB	BxKt (22) / RxB	QR-Ksq / R-Q5
20	P-KB4 / PxP+	KtxB / Kt-B4+	BxKt (11) / PxKt	PxP (17) / Kt-K2!	Kt-Kt4 / Q-K2 (23)	B-Kt3 / QRxKt(24)

Drawn.

For Notes see opposite page.

THE HAMPE-ALLGAIER-THOROLD GAMBIT.

A REVIVAL of interest has occurred in the Hampe-Allgaier Gambit; especially in what may be called the Hampe-Allgaier-Thorold. The text books have given the beauties and difficulties of this Opening but little attention. We present the substance of an analysis of it, by Mr W Timbrell Pierce, published in "The British Chess Magazine," 1884.

HAMPE-ALLGAIER-THOROLD GAMBIT.

1. P-K4 / P-K4 —— 2. Kt-QB3 / Kt-QB3 —— 3. P-B4 / PxP —— 4. Kt-B3 / P-KKt4 —— 5. P-KR4 / P-Kt5

	1	2	3	4	5	6
6	Kt-KKt5 / P-KR3 (1)				Kt-K4	P-Q3
7	KtxP / KxKt				P-Q4 / P-KR3	B-B4 / Kt-K4
8	P-Q4 / P-Q3 (2)			P-Q4	BxP (13) / Kt-Kt3	B-Kt3 / P-KR3
9	BxP (3) / B-Kt2			PxP / QKt-K2	KtxP / KxKt	P-Q4 / PxKt
10	B-B4ch / K-Kt3 (4)			B-B4 / K-Kt2	B-B4ch / P-Q4	PxKt (14)
11	B-K3 (5) / K-R2 (6)			BxP / Kt-KB3	KtxP— / —	
12	Q-Q3 (7) / KKt-K2 (8)	Castles / QxP		B-K5 / Kt-Kt3		
13	CastlesKR / Kt-Kt5 (9)	Q-Q3 / Kt-K2		P-R5 / KtxB		
14	Q-Q2 / P-Q4	P-K5ch / Kt-Kt3		PxKt / Kt-R2		
15	PxP / B-B4+	Kt-Q5 / P-Kt6	B-K3	Q-Q3 / Q-Kt4		
16		R-B7!+ (10)	QxKtch / KxQ	Kt-K4 / QxKP		
17			B-Q3ch / K-R4 (11)	CastlesKR / B-Q3		
18			Kt-B4ch / K-Kt4	KtxB / QxKt		
19			KtxBch / K-R4	QR-Ksq / R-Bsq!		
20			Ktmates.	RxR / KtxR (12)		

NOTES, to opposite page.

(1) If Black plays 6 P-B3, the following is likely : 7 QxP 7 P-KR4 (if 7 Kt-K4, 8 Q-R5ch 8 Kt-Kt3, 9 Kt-R3, &c.), 8 Q-B5 8 QKt-K2, 9 QxP(B4) 9 PxKt, 10 Q-K5 10 R-R3, 11 B-B4, with a strong attack.

(2) If 8 P-B6, **White proceeds 9 B-QB4ch, or 9 B-KB4 as in** the usual Allgaier, but with a better chance.

(3) White may check with B either on this **or the next move.** If White plays 9 B-B4ch Black should reply K-Kt3, in order to play B-Kt2.

(4) Better than K-Ksq, as the continuation then would be 11 B-K3 11 Q-K2, 12 Q-Q2, followed by CastlesQR, with a strong game.

(5) This move seems essential, to protect **the** QP.. White may, however, try 11 P-K5, **and** Black can hardly venture to take the P, because of the continuation 12 P-R5ch 12 K-B3 !, 13 B or PxPch, &c. Black's best reply is, probably, 11 B-B4, 12 P-R5ch 12 K-R2, 13 B-K6 13 KKt-K2, 14 BxBch 14 KtxB, 15 QxP, or Q-Q3. If Black reply 11 KKt-K2, White proceeds 12 P-R5ch 12 K-R2, 13 P-K6!, and Black has a difficult game. White **might also play,** with equal force, 11 P-R5ch, and 12 P-K5.

(6) Game, Zukertort v Hirschfeld. The object being to prevent White from Castling. **In another** game between the same players occurred this variation : 11 KKt-K2, 12 Castles 12 R-Bsq, 13 Q-Q2 13 K-R2, 14 RxR 14 QxR, 15 R-KBsq 15 Q-Ksq !, 16 B-B7 16 Q-Rsq !, 17 Kt-Q5 !+.

(7) Mr Pierce's latest opinion is that White's best course is to Castle (see next column).

(8) If Kt-Kt5, White wins with 13 P-K5ch.

(9) Best. If 13 R-Bsq, White continues 14 Kt-Q5, and wins.

(10) Threatening Kt-B6ch.

(11) If 17 B-B4, 18 RxB, with the better game, threatening R-R5ch, then if KxR, White mates in three.

(12) This, a correspondence game between Mr W T Pierce (White) and Mr **F** Budden (Black), was continued : 21 Q-QB3ch 21 K-B2, 22 R-Bsqch 22 K-Ksq (the move actually played was K-Ktsq, but the text move is stronger), 23 Q-Kt7 23 Q-K2, 24 Q-Kt8, **and** White should now recover his Piece and win, by B-Q3 and B-Kt6.

(13) PxKt is bad, for then ensues 8 PxKt, 9 QxP 9 P-Q3, 10 Q-Qsq (of course **White cannot** take KtP with Q) 10 PxKP, with much the better game.

(14) **And** Black appears to have the advantage slightly. Black cannot very **well capture** KP, **because of 11** BxPch 11 K-K2, 12 QxQch 12 KxQ. 13 BxKt 13 RxB, 14 PxP 14 RxP ?, 15 R-R8 15 K-Ksq, 16 Kt-Q5 +

HAMPE-ALLGAIER-THOROLD GAMBIT.

1. $\dfrac{\text{P-K4}}{\text{P-K4}}$
2. $\dfrac{\text{Kt-QB3}}{\text{Kt-QB3}}$
3. $\dfrac{\text{P-B4}}{\text{PxP}}$
4. $\dfrac{\text{Kt-B3}}{\text{P-KKt4}}$
5. $\dfrac{\text{P-KR4}}{\text{P-Kt5}}$
6. $\dfrac{\text{Kt-KKt5}}{\text{P-KR3}}$
7. $\dfrac{\text{KtxP}}{\text{KxKt}}$
8. $\dfrac{\text{P-Q4}}{}$

	7	8	9	10	11	12
	London, 1881. Wayte Zukertort	New Orleans, 1884. Zukertort Ernst	Chicago, 1884. Zukertort Adair	St. Louis, 1884. Zukertort Haller	Correspondence Game. Monck Jarvis	London. Mephisto Tschigorin
8	P-Q3		P-Q4		P-B6	
9	B-B4ch		PxP		B-QB4ch	
	K-Kt3 (1)	K-Ksq	QKt-K2		K-Ksq?	K-Kt2
10	BxP (2)	BxP	B-B4		PxP	PxP
	B-Kt2	B-Kt2	K-Kt2		B-K2	B-K2
11	B-K3	B-K3 .	Castles	BxP	B-K3	B-K3
	K-R2	Q-K2	P-B6	Kt-Kt3	BxPch	BxPch
12	Q-Q3 (3)	Castles	PxP	B-K5ch	K-Q2	K-Q2
	KKt-K2	QxRP	P-Kt6	Kt-B3	P-Q3	P-Q4?
13	CastlesQR	R-B7	B-B4	Castles (8)	Q-K2 (12)	PxQP
	R-Bsq	P-Kt6	Kt-B4	KtxB	B-B3	Kt-R4?
14	QR-Bsq	RxB	B-K5ch	PxKt	Q-R2	B-Q3
	Kt-Kt5	Q-R7ch	Kt-B3	B-QB4ch	Q-K2	B-K2
15	Q-Q2	K-Bsq	Kt-K4	K-R2	Kt-Q5	PxP
	P-Q4	Q-R8ch	B-K2	Kt-K5	Q-Kt2	Kt-KB3
16	RxR	B-Ktsq	Q-Q2	P-KKt3	P-B3	BxPch
	BxR	Kt-B3!	R-Bsq	KtxKt	P-KR4	RxB
17	PxP	R-B7 (5)	Q-B4	PxKt	QR-KKtsq	P-Kt5+
	B-B4	Kt-KKt5!	K-R2	R-Bsq	K-Qsq	
18	R-Bsq	Kt-Q5	B-Q3	Q-Q2	PxP	
	Q-Q2	Kt-R7ch	Kt(B3)xP	B-Q2 (9)	QBxP	
19	P-R3	K-K2	Q-Kt4	P-K6	B-K2	
	KtxBP	B-Kt5ch	Kt(Q4)-K6	RxR	K-Q2	
20	B-Ktsq (4)	K-Q3	Q-R5	RxR	Q-B4	
	P-KR4!	BxQ	BxP	B-Ksq	R-QBsq	
21	RxB	KtxBPch	KR-Ksq	Q-B4	RxP	
	QxR	K-Qsq	Kt-Q4	Q-K2	RxR (13)	
22	B-Q3	RxB	R-K2	QxPch (10)	BxBch	
	B-R3	QxP	Kt-Kt5	K-Rsq	K-Qsq	
23	KxKt	B-Kt3	B-QB4	B-Q3	BxR+	
	BxQ+	Kt-B6 (6)	KtxQP (7)	Q-Kt2 (11)		

NOTES, to opposite page.

(1) Mr Potter, in notes to this game, expresses dissatisfaction with this move. He dislikes it equally in the Thorold-Allgaier, although upheld by Zukertort, Steinitz, and Wayte.

(2) The object here, as in Mr Thorold's variation of the Allgaier, is to clear the KB file for the R. Nevertheless, Mr Potter says, having regard to the position of the Black K, he prefers for White, 10 Kt-Q5, as putting a useful Piece in action, and anticipating Black's B-K2.

(3) Q-Q2 would be better.

(4) If 20 RxB 20 KtxB, 21 QxKt 21 KtxR, 22 B-Q3 22 B-Q3 !, 23 Q-B2 23 R-KBsq+.

(5) Mr Zukertort afterwards pronounced this weak, and said 17 Kt-Q5 might have maintained the attack. The variations, however, are very complicated. 17 RxP would be bad for White, on account of 17 R-Bsq, 18 Q-Q3 18 Kt-QKt5+.

(6) Continued, 24 B-K3 24 Kt-K4ch, 25 PxKt 25 KtxPch, 26 K-B3 26 KtxR, 27 KtxR 27 QxP, 28 BxQRP 28 K-K2, 29 Kt-Kt6 29 Q-K6ch, 30 R-Q3 30 Q-B4ch, 31 K-Q2 31 Q-R4ch, and White resigned.

(7) Continued, 24 R-Q2 24 KtxKBPch, 25 QxKt 25 RxQ, 26 RxQ 26 BxR, and White resigned.

(8) Mr Ranken says this is an error, and that White should have played instead, P-R5.

(9) But now Black in his turn is faulty. He ought to plant the B at KB4, and on White's playing R-B4, in order to double his Rooks, the Q might go to Ksq, and afterward to Kt3.

(10) Mr Ranken thinks Q-K5ch would have given White an advantage.

(11) Continued, 24 Q-K4 24 B-Q3, 25 R-B3 25 B-R4, 26 R-K3 26 B-B4, 27 R-K2 27 BxR, and White resigned.

(12) PxP would be dangerous, on account of B-Kt4.

(13) BxR, giving up the Q, would be better.

THE STEINITZ GAMBIT. THE FYFE GAMBIT.

THE Steinitz Gambit, formerly considered a remarkable combination of ingenuity and bold movement of the King, has doubtless met its fate in a simple discovery by the Rev G A MacDonnell, that Black, in the opening moves, has the option of forcing a draw. Mr Steinitz has hardly yet conceded the downfall of the Gambit; but his attempted vindication of it in the London Congress had a disastrous effect on his score.

THE Fyfe Gambit, which is not referred to in the "Synopsis," was introduced early in 1883 by Mr Fyfe, of the Glasgow Chess Club. Mr Blackburne gave it a brief examination, during a visit to Glasgow, and is said to have expressed the opinion that the Gambit leads to an even game.

NOTES, to opposite page.

(A) The Rev C E Ranken says (1884): "This move undoubtedly, in our opinion, initiates the true defence to the Steinitz Gambit, for if now PxP, it enables Black to draw, if he pleases, by Q-K2ch, &c.; or to institute, as the game (Col 3) exemplifies, a severe, if not fatal attack, at the temporary cost of a Piece. If, on the other hand, KtxP, Black obtains a decisive advantage by 6 B-KKt5ch, 7 Kt-B3 7 Castles, 8 P-B3 (or BxP) 8 P-B4, &c.

(1) This repetition of checks by the Q, alternately at KR5 and K2, has apparently demolished the Steinitz Gambit as an attack. White must either concede a draw at this early stage, or take very hazardous risks.

(2) This assuming of the risks referred to, in a great International contest, was plucky, at all events.

(3) 9 KtxP, 10 PxP 10 Q-Kt5, is recommended by Dr Zukertort, among others, as a more simple and safer line of play. Mr Steinitz says White should play 9 Q-Ksqch, followed by PxP.

(4) A losing move. Q-K2ch is best.

(5) If 14 Q-K4ch, Black's best reply is Q-K2.

(6) Continued, 21 RxKt 21 QxKt, 22 Q-R4 22 P-KR4, 23 R-KKt3 23 KR-Ksq, 24 RxB 24 Q-Q8ch, 25 K-R2 25 QxQR, 26 QxQ 26 PxQ, 27 K-Kt3 27 QR-Qsq, 28 BxP 28 R-K7, 29 P-Kt4 29 RxP, 30 R-Ksq 30 R-Q6ch, 31 K-R4 31 P-Kt3, 32 R-K7 32 P-Kt6, 33 R-Ksq 33 R-Q5ch, 34 KxP 34 RxP, and White resigned.

(7) Not so good, Mr Steinitz says, as Kt-B3.

(8) Mr Steinitz condemns this as very weak, and regards Kt-KB3 as the proper move, leading to a strong attack; but these suggestions have not been fully tested.

(9) Continued, 21 B-B4 21 P-Kt4!, 22 BxQPch 22 K-Kt2, 23 RxB 23 KtxR, 24 Q-B3ch 24 P-B3, 25 R-KBsq 25 Q-K5ch, 26 K-Ktsq 26 Q-K7, 27 R-B3 27 KR-Ksq!, 28 BxR 28 RxB, 29 B-B5 29 Q-R7ch, 30 K-Bsq 30 R-K7, and White resigned. Mr Minchin says, in the Book of the Congress, that the result of these two games, at his own Opening, severely handicapped Mr Steinitz. Whether the Gambit be or be not, he continues, theoretically sound, the danger in endeavouring to avoid the perpetual check on the eighth move was so great practically, that even Mr Steinitz, who is so thoroughly acquainted with all its intricacies, did not again venture to adopt it, and it will probably never again be played in important contests, or only by an inferior player, content to accept the draw, which the second player can force.

(10) The Fyfe Gambit, which has not yet been carefully analysed. "The Glasgow Weekly Herald" pronounces it worthy of attention.

(11) A hampering move to Black.

(12) Perhaps the capture of the Kt would have been better.

(13) Continued, 21 P-KKt5 21 RPxP, 22 PxP 22 R-R2, 23 PxP 23 PxP, 24 B-Kt8! 24 R-R5, 25 R-Kt7ch 25 K-Qsq, 26 QR-KKtsq 26 RxP, 27 B-K6, and Black resigned.

(14) Continued, 21 QxQ 21 PxQ, 22 BxPch 22 K-K2, 23 B-Q5 23 B-B3, 24 P-B4?, and to this weak move White attributed the ultimate loss of the game.

(15) Though White's Pawns are in a ragged state, Black's game is almost wholly undeveloped.

(16) If White wins the P, Black can force an exchange of Queens.

(17) Continued, 21 RxBP 21 K-K2, 22 QR-Bsq (not good, but Black failed to see the winning reply, Kt-B4) 22 B-Q2, 23 RxRP, and Black's oversight led to the loss of the game.

STEINITZ GAMBIT.   FYFE GAMBIT.

	1	2	3	1	2	3
	London 1883 Congress. Steinitz Englisch	London 1883 Congress. Steinitz Tschigorin	Germantown, Pa., 1883. Steinitz Shipley	Glasgow, 1883.	Glasgow, 1883.	Glasgow, 1883.
				Spens and Fyfe versus Crum and Thomson each game.		
1	P-K4 / P-K4			P-K4 / P-K4		
2	Kt-QB3 / Kt-QB3			Kt-QB3 / Kt-QB3		
3	P-B4 / PxP			P-Q4 (10) / KtxP		
4	P-Q4 / Q-R5ch			P-B4 / B-Kt5		
5	K-K2 / P-Q4 (A)			Kt-B3 / Kt-QB3		BxKtch
6	PxP / Q-K2ch		B-KKt5ch	P-B5 (11) / Kt-B3		PxB / KtxKt
7	K-B2 / Q-R5ch (1)		Kt-B3 / Castles	B-KKt5 / P-Q3		QxKt / PxP
8	P-KKt3 (2) / PxPch		PxKt / B-QB4	P-QR3 / B-R4 (12)		BxP (15) / Kt-K2
9	K-Kt2 / B-Q3 (3)		PxPch / K-Ktsq	P-QKt4 / B-Kt3		Q-Kt3 / Kt-Kt3 (16)
10	PxKt (4) / PxRP	Q-Ksqch / QKt-K2	Kt-QKt5 / Kt-B3	Kt-Q5 / Kt-Q5		BxP / Q-R5
11	Q-B3 / PxKt(Q)ch	PxP / QxQP	K-Q3 / B-B4ch	KtxKt(Q4) / BxKt	KtxB / KtxKtch	QxQ / KtxQ
12	KxQ / QxPch	R-R4 (7) / Q-B3	K-B3 / Kt-K5ch	P-B3 / B-B7ch!	QxKt / RPxKt	B-Q6! / K-Qsq
13	B-K3 / Q-B3	Kt-K4 / Q-Kt3	K-Kt3 / Q-B3	K-K2 / KtxKt!	B-QB4 / B-Q2	B-QB4 / R-Ksq
14	Q-K2 (5) / Kt-K2	B-Q3 / B-KB4	Q-Ksq / KR-Ksq	BxQ / KtxPch	CastlesKR / P-B3	CastlesKR / P-B3
15	B-Kt2 / PxP	KtxBch (8) / PxKt	B-Q3 / BxP	KxB / KtxQch	KR-Qsq / P-Kt4	B-KB7 / RxP
16	Kt-K4 / Q-Kt3	B-QKt5ch / K-Bsq!	KKtxB / Kt-B4ch	RxKt / KxB	B-Kt3 / Q-Kt3ch	QR-Ksq / Kt-B4!
17	P-B4 / B-KKt5	P-B4 / Kt-KB3	K-B4 / RxQ	B-B4 / P-KB3	K-Rsq / P-B4	B-KB4 / R-K3
18	Q-KB2 / CastlesKR	Kt-B3 / B-Kt5	RxR / KtxB	P-Kt4 / K-K2	BxKt / PxB	P-Kt4 / Kt-R5
19	R-Ksq / Kt-B4	Kt-Q4 / Kt-B4	PxKt / P-QR3	P-KR4 / P-KR3	Q-K3 / R-R3	BxR / PxB
20	KtxB / KtxB (6)	KtxKt / QxKt (9)	P-QR4 / PxKtch+	KR-Ktsq / B-Q2 (13)	PxP / QxP (14)	B-R6? / PxB (17)

For Notes see opposite page.

H

THE ENGLISH OPENING.

THE " Synopsis " gives a few illustrative extracts from games at this Opening, remarking of it only that it is calculated to bring about positions in which each side is soon thrown upon its own resources.

No doubt this is a correct opinion, and the fact is the main reason why the English Opening has been so frequently played of late in tournaments and matches. We find quite a number of examples of it in the Vienna Congress of 1882, and the London Congress of 1883. It was played in the telegraphic match between Liverpool and Calcutta, 1881, and was the Opening chosen by Vienna in one of the pending games with Paris. There is evidently a growing faith in its merits as a solid and cautious Opening, a faith that has had a quiet development, but that is striking, after a review of recent important contests.

The " Chess Player's Chronicle " says the Opening is safe, sound, and satisfactory, and is frequently resorted to where a stern and determined struggle is expected. Mr Bird said, in 1883, that it is equal to any Opening on the board.

M. Rosenthal has proposed to meet White's 1 P-QB4 with 1 P-K4, in order to bring about an open game; but Mr Steinitz's judgment is adverse to the experiment.

ENGLISH OPENING.

	1	2	3	4	5	6
	Telegraph Match, 1881. Liverpool Calcutta	Vienna 1882 Congress. Steinitz Mackenzie	London 1883 Congress. Mason Zukertort	London 1863 Congress. Zukertort Blackburne	Telegraph Match, 1884. Vienna Paris	Vienna Club Tourney 1882 Hruby Schwarz
1	P-QB4					P-K4 (13)
	P-K3 (1)					
2	P-K3		Kt-KB3		P-Q4	P-K3
	P-QB4				P-Q4	Kt-KB3
3	P-QKt3	P-Q4	Kt-KB3		Kt-QB3	Kt-QB3
	P-Q4 (2)	P-Q4	P-Q4	P-QKt3	Kt-KB3	P-Q4
4	Kt-KB3	PxBP	P-Q4	B-K2	Kt-B3	PxP
	P-Q5 (3)	BxP	B-K2	B-Kt2	B-K2	KtxP
5	B-Kt2	PxP	Kt-B3	Castles	P-K3	Kt-B3
	Kt-QB3	PxP	Castles	P-Q4	Castles	P-KB3 (14)
6	P-QKt4 (4)	Kt-KB3	B-Q3	P-Q4	B-K2	B-B4
	QPxP (5)	Kt-QB3	P-QKt3	B-Q3	P-QKt3	KtxKt (15)
7	BPxP	B-Q3	PxP	Kt-B3	Castles	KtPxKt
	KtxP	Kt-B3	PxP	Castles	B-Kt2	B-Q3
8	P-Q4	Castles	Kt-K5	P-QKt3	P-QKt3	P-Q4
	Kt-KB3	Castles	B-Kt2	QKt-Q2	QKt-Q2	PxP
9	P-QR3	QKt-Q2	Castles	B-Kt2	B-Kt2	BPxP
	Kt-R3 (6)	B-Kt3	P-B4	Q-K2	P-B4	Q-K2
10	B-Q3	P-QR3	B-Q2	Kt-B3	B-Q3	Q-Kt3
	P-QKt3	Kt-K2	Kt-B3	Kt-K5	Kt-K5	Kt-B3
11	Castles	P-QKt4	KtxKt	KtxB	BPxP	B-Q2
	PxP	B-KB4	BxKt	PxKt	KtxKt	Kt-Qsq
12	PxP	Kt-Kt3 .	R-Bsq	Kt-Q2	BxKt	CastlesKR
	B-Kt2	Kt-K5	P-B5	QKt-B3	BxP	Kt-B2
13	Kt-B3	B-Kt2	B-Ktsq	P-B3	P-K4	P-K4!
	Kt-B2	Kt-Kt3	P-QKt4	KtxKt	B-Kt2	P-B3
14	B-B2	KKt-Q4 (8)	Kt-K2	QxKt	R-Ksq	P-K5
	Kt-Q2	B-Q2	P-Kt5	PxP	PxP	PxP (16)
15	B-R4	R-Bsq	Kt-Kt3	BxP	BxP	PxP
	P-B3	R-Bsq	P-QR4	P-Q4	B-B4	B-QB4
16	Kt-K5+ (7)	RxR	R-Ksq	B-Q3	B-Kt2	P-K6
		BxR	P-R5	KR-Bsq	Q-K2	Kt-Q3
17		Q-B2	Kt-B5	QR-Ksq	Game in	B-KKt5
		Q-K2	P-R6	R-B2	progress.	Q-QB2
18		R-Bsq	P-K4	P-K4		QR-Qsq
		P-B4 (9)	RPxP	QR-QBsq		P-KR3
19		Kt-B5	R-B2	P-K5		B-R4
		BxKt	B-R5 (10)	Kt-Ksq		P-KKt4
20		PxB+	P-K5	P-B4		B-Kt3
			Kt-Ksq (11)	P-Kt3 (12)		Q-K2 (17)

For Notes see page 61.

ENGLISH OPENING.

	7	8	9	10	11	12
	London 1883 Congress.	London 1883 Congress.	Vienna 1882 Congress.	London 1883 Congress.	Vienna 1882 Congress.	London 1883 Congress.
	Skipworth Steinitz	Skipworth Winawer	Hruby Mason	Mackenzie Mortimer	Mason Tschigorin	Mason Sellman
1	P-QB4					P-QB4
	P-K4 (18)		P-KB4			
2	P-K3		P-K3			P-K3
	P-KKt3	Kt-QB3	Kt-KB3		P-K3	P-K3
3	Kt-QB3	P-QR3	Kt-QB3	Kt-KB3	Kt-QB3	Kt-KB3
	B-Kt2	P-KKt3	P-K3	Kt-B3	Kt-KB3	P-Q4
4	B-K2 (19)	Kt-QB3	P-Q4 (22)	P-Q4	P-Q4	P-Q4
	Kt-K2	B-Kt2	B-K2	P-K3	P-QKt3	Kt-KB3
5	P-Q3	P-Q3	B-Q3	P-QR3	Kt-B3	Kt-B3
	Castles	P-Q3	P-QKt3	Kt-K2	B-Kt2	Kt-B3
6	Kt-B3	B-K2	Kt-R3	Kt-B3	P-KKt3	PxQP
	P-Q4	P-B4	B-Kt2	P-B3	B-Kt5	KKtxP [29]
7	Castles	B-Q2	Castles	B-Q3	B-Kt2	B-Kt5
	QKt-B3	QKt-K2	Castles	Kt-Kt3	Castles	KtxKt
8	P-K4	Q-B2	P-B3	Q-K2 (25)	Castles	PxKt
	PxBP	P-B3	Kt-B3	P-Q4	BxQKt	B-Q2
9	PxP	Kt-B3	P-R3	P-B5	PxB	Castles
	Kt-Q5	Kt-B3	K-Rsq	B-K2	P-Q4	B-K2
10	B-K3	P-K4	P-QKt4	P-QKt4	Kt-K5 (27)	B-Q2
	P-KR3	Castles	Q-Ksq	Q-B2	QKt-Q2	Castles
11	Q-Q2	P-KR4	R-R2	P-Kt3	P-B4	Q-K2
	K-R2	P-KR3	P-QR4	P-K4!	P-B4	Q-B2
12	QR-Qsq	CastlesQR	P-Kt5	PxP	PxQP	B-Q3
	Kt(K2)-B3	Q-B2	Kt-Qsq	KtxP	KtxP	P-QR3 (30)
13	Kt-Q5	K-Ktsq	P-K4 (23)	KtxKt	Q-Kt3	KR-Bsq
	Kt-K3	B-K3	PxP	QxKt	KtxKt	KR-Bsq
14	B-Q3	QR-Bsq	PxP	B-Kt2	BPxKt	Kt-Ksq
	Kt(B3)-Q5	P-Q4	P-K4	Q-B2	P-QB5	P-QKt4
15	KtxKt (20)	Q-Bsq	P-Q5	Q-B2	Q-B2 (28)	P-KB4
	PxKt	QPxKP	B-B4ch	P-KKt3	Q-Q2	P-Kt3
16	B-B4	PxP	K-Rsq	Kt-K2	B-Q2	Kt-B3
	P-QB3	PxP	P-Q3	R-Bsq	KR-Qsq	P-B5
17	Kt-Kt4	Kt-KR2	Kt-R4	Kt-Q4	P-K4	B-K4
	KtxB	P-KR4	B-Bsq	Kt-K5	Kt-Kt5	P-B4?
18	QxKt	Kt-Qsq	KtxB	P-B3	Q-Qsq	B-B2
	Q-Kt3	Kt-B4	BxKt	Kt-Kt4	PxP	B-R6
19	P-QR3	B-Kt5	PxB	K-B2	B-Kt5	KR-Ktsq
	P-QR4	Kt-Q5	KtPxKt	B-Q2	Kt-Q4	Kt-Qsq
20	Kt-B2	Q-B2? (21)	QR-KB2	P-KR4?	BxR+	Kt-K5
	QxP+	KtxQ+	Kt-Q2 (24)	Kt-K5ch! [26]		B-Ksq (31)

For Notes see page 61.

NOTES, to pages 59 and 60.

(1) "The Chess Player's Chronicle" says this is conceded to be the best reply, though many excellent players adopt P-KB4.

(2) Though the "Chronicle" urges nothing specific against this, it prefers one of the following moves: Kt-KB3, Kt-QB3, B-K2.

(3) A dangerous advance. One of the Knights should have been played.

(4) Well played. Liverpool gets more than an equivalent in position.

(5) Ill judged. The opening of the B file must greatly increase White's facilities for attack. KtxP was a better move.

(6) The "Chronicle" says this Kt should have gone to B3, and eventually to KKt3, if possible, but it seems the Calcutta players failed to consider Castling as a means of escape from their embarrasment, and that they supposed the extra P would compensate them for any inferiority in other respects.

(7) Calcutta did well to resign. If the Kt be taken immediately, White checks with Q, and captures the KP. Black might have delayed the result by 16 P-QKt4, but White had a winning position several moves back.

(8) The beginning of a vigorous attack.

(9) This move weakens the QP.

(10) Forced, to save a Piece.

(11) The game ran up to 73 moves, and was won by Black, though White missed a draw, and possibly a win.

(12) The remaining moves of this game, which is undoubtedly the most brilliant played at the Congress, were 21 R-K3! 21 P-B4, 22 PxP en pass 22 KtxP, 23 P-B5! 23 Kt-K5, 24 BxKt 24 PxB, 25 PxKtP 25 R-B7, 26 PxPch 26 K-Rsq, 27 P-Q5ch 27 P-K4, 28 Q-K4! 28 R(Bsq)-B4, 29 R-B8ch 29 KxP, 30 QxPch 30 K-Kt2, 31 BxPch 31 KxR, 32 B-Kt7ch 32 K-Ktsq, 33 QxQ, and Black resigned.

(13) This idea of M Rosenthal's looking to an open game has received as yet no encouragement from other analysts.

(14) This move makes Black's game inferior. Mr Steinitz says KtxKt, followed by B-Q3, was the only plausible continuation. Black could not advance the KP, after KtxKt, on account of the ultimate rejoinder, Q-QR4ch.

(15) A move that aids White to form his centre. Kt-Kt3, attacking the B, was better.

(16) If B-B2, White replies 15 B-Kt4, with fatal effect.

(17) Continued, 21 Q-Q3! 21 P-Kt4, 22 Q-Kt6ch 22 K-Qsq, 23 RxKtch! 23 BxR, 24 R-Qsq, and Black resigned.

(18) In notes to this game, Mr Steinitz says this reply is not much favored by book authorities or first-class practitioners. He adopted it here in order to continue it with an experiment on the next move.

(19) Mr Steinitz prefers Kt-B3.

(20) This loses a P; but, in any event, Mr Steinitz considers that Black has a slight superiority of position.

(21) A blunder due to ill health.

(22) A position identical with one in the Hollandish Opening.

(23) Mr Sellman says White's conduct of the Opening is much to be admired.

(24) Continued, 21 Q-R5! 21 Kt-Kt2? (P-Kt3 was the only hope of prolonging the game), and White won.

(25) The Q has no effect on this square. Castles, followed by P-QKt4 and B-Kt2, is better.

(26) Mr Mortimer had the game in his hands at the 38th move, but through errors, lost it on the 62nd move.

(27) White has opened with skill.

(28) If QxP, Black's reply is R-Bsq.

(29) Mr Mason says it is the usage of late for Black to take the P with Kt, in order to avoid the isolation of his QP.

(30) Preparatory to advancing the KtP. Black's position on the Q side is stronger than that of his opponent.

(31) 21 P-K4. Mr Mason says, in a note to this move, that whether Black capture the P or not, it is clear that White's game has improved, owing to Black's 17th move. Black resigned the game on the 40th move.

CENTRE GAMBIT.

	1	2	3	4	5	6
	Correspond. Match, 1884.	Vienna 1882 Congress.	Consultation Game.	Nash Corresp Tourney 1884	Vienna 1882 Congress.	Paris, 1883.
	Glasgow Edinburgh	Tschigorin Mackenzie	Berlin 1881 Congress.	Budden Blake	Winawer Tschigorin	Boistertre De Rivière
1	P-K4 / P-K4					
2	P-Q4 / PxP					
3	QxP / Kt-QB3				Q-B3 (20)	P-QB3 / PxP (22)
4	Q-K3 / Kt-B3	P-KKt3		B-Kt5ch	Q-K3 / Kt-B3	B-QB4 / P-B7 (23)
5	P-K5 / Kt-Q4	B-Q2 / B-Kt2	Kt-QB3 (11) / B-Kt2	P-QB3 / B-R4	Kt-QB3 / Kt-Q5	QxP / Kt-QB3 (24)
6	Q-K4 / KKt-K2	Kt-QB3 / P-Q3	Kt-Q5 (12) / P-Q3	Q-Kt3 / Q-B3	B-Q3 / B-B4	Q-Kt3 (25) / Q-B3
7	Kt-QB3 / Kt-Kt3	P-B4 / KKt-K2	Kt-K2 / KKt-K2	P-KB4 / P-Q3	Q-Kt3 / Kt-K2	Kt-KB3 / B-B4
8	P-B4 / B-Kt5	Castles / B-K3	B-Q2 / Castles (13)	B-Q3 / B-Kt3	B-KB4 / Kt-K3	Kt-B3 / KKt-K2
9	B-Q2 / Castles	Kt-B3 / Q-Q2	Castles / KtxKt	Kt-B3 / KKt-K2	B-K3 / BxB	Castles / Castles
10	Castles / P-B4 (1)	Kt-Q5 / CastlesQR	PxKt / Kt-K2	QKt-Q2 / B-Q2	QxB / Kt-B5	B-KKt5 / Q-Kt3
11	Q-B4ch / K-Rsq	B-B3 / BxB	B-B3 / Kt-B4	Kt-B4 / Q-Kt3	B-Bsq / Castles	B-Q3 / P-Q3
12	P-KR4 (2) / BxKt	QxB / Kt-QKt1 (9)	Q-Q3 (14) / Q-R5	P-B5 / QxQ	P-KKt3 / Kt(B5)-Kt3	BxKt / KtxB
13	QxB (3) / KKt-K2	Q-R3 / BxKt	P-KKt3 / Q-R5	PxQ / Kt-R4 (17)	Castles / P-QR3	Kt-Q5 (26) / KtxKt
14	B-B4 / P-QR3	PxB / Q-B4	K-Ktsq / P-B4	Kt-Kt5 (18) / P-KB3	P-B4 / P-Kt4	QxKt / P-QB3
15	Kt-R3 / Q-Ksq (4)	P-KKt3 / KtxP	P-R4 / P-B5	KtxRP! / K-B2 (19)	P-KR4 / P-Kt5	Q-Kt3 / B-KR6
16	B-Kt3 (5) / Kt-KKtsq	Kt-Q4! / Q-Q2	Q-Q2 / B-R3	KtxKt / BxKt	QKt-K2 / Q-K3	Kt-Ksq / P-Kt4
17	P-Kt4 (6) / PxP	Kt-Kt5 / P-QB3	Kt-B4 / P-QKt4	P-KKt4! / P-KKt4	P-R5 / Kt-Rsq	K-Rsq / B-K3
18	Kt-Kt5 / Kt-R3	KtxRPch / K-B2	P-KKt4 (15) / P-Kt5 (16)	BxP+	P-R6 / Kt-B4	Q-B2 / P-B4
19	P-R5 / R-B4 (7)	RxKt! / PxR	BxKtP / BxKt		Q-B5 / KtxRP	P-K5 / B-Q4
20	KR-Ksq / QxRP (8)	B-Kt5 / Q-K3 (10)	QxB / QxB+		QxKtP / P-R4 (21)	P-KB4 / QR-Qsq+

For Notes see opposite page.

NOTES, to opposite page.

(1) This opens up Black's position to attack, but it is doubtful if he has a better move.

(2) The P obviously cannot be taken.

(3) It was necessary to take the B with the Q, because 13 BxB 13 P-Kt4, followed by KtxBP, gives Black as good a game as White, if not better.

(4) At this stage QKtP or QRP might have been advanced.

(5) It is necessary to keep the B on this diagonal.

(6) The winning move. It is dangerous to take or leave the Pawn.

(7) White threatens Q-Q3.

(8) Not a good move. Black evidently did not notice the smothered mate variation if R was retired to Bsq. The remaining moves of this game, which was brilliantly played by White, were: 21 R-Rsq 21 Q-Kt3, 22 RxKt 22 PxR, 23 P-K6ch 23 R-B3, 24 Kt-B7ch, and Black resigned. If 24 K-Kt2, 25 P-B5 and wins. If 24 K-Ktsq, 25 P-K7 and wins.

(9) As White threatens Kt-B6.

(10) Continued, 21 Q-B3ch 21 K-Kt3, 22 R-Ksq 22 KxKt, 23 RxQ+.

(11) White was played by L Paulsen, Riemann, and Schallop, and Black by Blackburne, Minckwitz, and Schwarz.

(12) The Kt cannot be dislodged here.

(13) BxP would be bad, for then follows 9 P-QB3 9 BxR, 10 Kt-B6ch, &c.

(14) B3 would probably be a better post for the Q.

(15) A losing move. P-QKt3 should have been played.

(16) This loses a P, but leads to a fine attack.

(17) P-B3 is the move.

(18) Threatening KtxKt, followed by B-B4.

(19) A mistaken attempt to win a Piece. The proper move was Castles.

(20) An unusual move, proposed by Mr Paulsen.

(21) Continued, 21 Q-Q4 21 R-Ktsq (White wins speedily if Black captures RP, by 22 Kt-QB3, &c.), 22 Kt-QB3 22 R-Kt5, 23 Q-B5 23 B-Kt2, 24 Kt-B3 24 R-Ktsq, 25 P-R3 25 RxKtP, 26 KxR 26 BxPch, 27 B-Kt5 27 BxKt, 28 QxP 28 R-KBsq, 29 KR-Ksq 29 Q-Kt5, 30 RxP 30 QxKtP, 31 R-Q8 31 P-Kt3?, 32 RxRch 32 KxR, 33 R-K8ch, and Black resigned.

(22) M Rosenthal says he prefers this to Q-K2 or P-Q4, which only equalise the game.

(23) The same authority recommends this move, as it preserves Black's advantage of a P.

(24) The correct move is B-Kt5ch.

(25) Kt-KB3 is better.

(26) Weak. He should have played Kt-QKt5, followed by P-K5, to break Black's centre Pawns.

CENTRE COUNTER GAMBIT.

	1	2	3	4	5	6
	Vienna 1882 Congress. Mason Schwarz	New Orleans, 1884. Zukertort McConnell	New Orleans, 1884. Zukertort Maurian			
1	P-K4 / P-Q4					
2	PxP / QxP					
3	Kt-QB3 / Q-K4ch (1)	Q-Qsq			Q-QR4	Q-Q3 (10)
4	B-K2 / P-QB3 (2)	Kt-B3 / B-Kt5	P-K3	P-Q4 (7) / P-KKt3	P-Q4 / P-QB3	Kt-Kt5 / Q-K4ch
5	Kt-B3 / Q-B2	B-B4 (4) / P-K3	P-Q4 / Kt-KB3	B-K3 / B-Kt2	Kt-B3 / B-B4 (9)	B-K2 / Kt-QR3
6	P-Q4 / B-B4?	P-Q4 / B-Q3	B-Q3 / B-K2	Q-Q2 (8)		Kt-KB3 / Q-B3
7	P-Q5 / B-Q2	Castles / P-KR3	Castles / Castles			P-Q4 / P-R3
8	Castles / P-K3	Q-K2 / Kt-KB3	Kt-K2 / P-QKt3			
9	PxKP / BxP	Kt-Qsq / B-KB4	P-B3 / B-Kt2			
10	Kt-Q4 / Kt-B3	Kt-K3 / B-K5	Q-B2 / P-Kt3 (6)			
11	KtxB / PxKt	Kt-Q2 / QKt-Q2	B-R6 / R-Ksq			
12	B-QB4 / P-K4	KtxB / KtxKt	Kt-Kt3 / QKt-Q2			
13	P-B4 / B-Q3	B-Q3 / KKt-B3	QR-Qsq / Kt-Kt5			
14	R-Ksq / QKt-Q2	P-QB4 / P-B4?	B-K3 / B-Q3			
15	PxP / BxP	Kt-B5 / B-Bsq	Kt-K4 / B-K2			
16	P-KKt3 / CastlesQR	P-Q5 / P-KKt3	P-KR3 / KtxB			
17	Q-B3 / QR-Ksq	PxP / PxKt!	PxKt / Kt-B3			
18	B-K3 / KR-Bsq	PxKtch / KxP	KtxKt / KBxKt			
19	QR-Qsq / P-KR4	BxPch / K-B3	P-K4 / Q-K2			
20	B-B4 / BxB (3)	Q-B3ch / K-B2 (5)	P-K5 / B-Kt4			
			Drawn game.			

For Notes see opposite page.

NOTES, to opposite page.

(1) Inferior to Q-R4.

(2) B-Kt5 is the usual play.

(3) White should have scored this game, but Black managed to creep out of his difficulties, and won on the 52nd move.

(4) An unorthodox move.

(5) Continued, 21 B-B4ch 21 B-Q3, 22 QR-Qsq 22 Kt-Ksq, 23 R-Q5 23 P-Kt3, 24 KR-Qsq, and Black resigned.

(6) BxKt would have been imprudent.

(7) The analysis in this and succeeding columns are from "Land and Water," which says of the Centre Counter Gambit: "This Defence stands condemned by analysts, and tabooed by players. We must admit that there is something suspicious about it, but at any rate it is a fighting defence, and one far removed from drawish tendencies. When Mr W N Potter had to play his nineteenth game against Mr Mason in their match, the former could not afford any draws, for the score then stood: Mason 5, Potter 3, draws 10. By reason of draws above the number of eight counting as half to each player, the score was really 6 to 4, and two more draws would have given Mr Mason the match. Mr Potter chose then to rely upon a Centre Counter, and with good effect; so much so, indeed, that when the twenty-first game was played, Mr Mason chose a Van't Kruys, with the expressed object of avoiding another Centre Counter Gambit. This instance shows that the Defence is at least playable between strong players; and, perhaps, were it oftener adopted, its claims as a regular Opening might become recognised."

(8) "White has the advantage, but if Black had played 4 P-QB3, 5 Kt-B3, 6 B-B4 6 B-K2, or 6 B-QB4 6 P-K3, we should doubt if White's superiority, though not to be denied, is at all striking."

(9) "Or P-KKt3, with an almost even game. Instead of 4 P-QB3, Black may, like Anderssen against Morphy, play 4 P-K4, whereupon 5 PxP 5 QxPch, 6 B-K2 6 B-QKt5, and although we cannot allow that Black is quite all right, yet we will not put ourselves so far in contradiction with those who take that view, as to deny that there is plenty of fighting in his game. However, after 3 Q-QR4, Zukertort recommends 4 Kt-KB3, which he considers prevents 4 P-K4, for then 5 B-Kt5ch 5 P-B3, 6 B-B4. Here the given reply for Black is B-KB4, but we would rather rely upon B-K2, though we do not pretend that we relish, in either case, the effects of 4 P-K4. The question arises whether the two replies, 3 Q-Qsq and 3 Q-QR4, comprise all that Black can attempt. This we are far from thinking. Mr Mason, not long since, played 3 Q-K4ch, and we do not know that any very dreadful disaster came, in consequence, upon Black's game. 3 Q-Q2 looks about as bad a move as could be made, but anyone trying to demonstrate it, might not find the proof very easy. Suppose White play 4 Kt-B3, and Black, regardless of consequences, respond with P-KKt3, what would come of it? Nothing, save that White would have rather the better game, which is an old story, and one that could just as well be told of many variations of other Openings, even though analysts callously say, at the end, 'even game.' If the analysts were asked to accept such equality as the basis of a real game, with a good round stake upon it, we should probably find a display of practical modesty such as would be very edifying in its way."

(10) "We consider 3 Q-QR4 to be the best of the continuations, but we rather fancy that there is another quite as good, viz., 3 Q-Q3, which directly intends the move striven against by analysts and players, namely, P-K4. Now, how can White prevent that advance? 4 P-Q4 is no hindrance, while 4 Kt-K4 is obviously futile, even if Black answer with no other move than Q-K4, though various other good answers are open to him. As to 4 Kt-Kt5, that continuation will assist Black's development, even if he should now take his Queen straight back to her own square, though he might play instead Q-K4ch—(see Col 6). Altogether, we consider that the Centre Counter Gambit deserves much more consideration than it has hitherto received."

THE SICILIAN DEFENCE.

THE frequent employment of this Defence in former years, was due to Mr Staunton's opinion that it was the best Opening the second player could adopt. This estimate has not been sustained. In fact the Sicilian has now scarcely the standing of a first-class Defence. The result of the Sicilian games at the London Congress was against the Opening. Mr Potter, who has thoroughly tested the Sicilian in important contests, said of it (in "Land and Water") in 1884 :

"The sympathy we feel towards defendants secures for this Opening our best wishes ; but we cannot allow our judgment to be swayed by desire, and there is that about the Sicilian which causes us to have the strongest doubts concerning its soundness as a Defence. 1 P-K4 1 P-QB4, 2 Kt-QB3 2 Kt-QB3, 3 Kt-B3 3 P-K3, 4 P-Q4 4 PxP, 5 KtxP. Surveying the board at this, the critical phase of the Opening, there can be no question but that Black's game looks highly unpromising. Both 5 Kt-B3 and 5 B-Kt5 have been found unsatisfactory, and the same as to any other move of a developing kind, so that, after the rise and fall of many hopes, the tendency is to return to the old love, viz., 5 P-QR3, but White now plays 6 B-K2, after which let us again look at the board. White has three Pieces in the field, and is able to Castle, while his QB is almost in as good play as if already on the field, and he has a clear Queen's file. In other words, White's game is in a highly developed condition, and for this advantage he has neither given up a Gambit Pawn, nor made any other kind of payment. On Black's side, we see but one Piece in the field, and none of the other Pieces can be speedily developed in any useful fashion. The QB is dreadfully blocked up, and the QP dangerously weak. We are also constrained to look curiously upon one special feature—namely, that in the three lines of Black's position there is but one white square unoccupied, viz., KKt3, as against eight black squares similarly unoccupied. Those occupied white squares imply a very confined, locked-up position ; whilst, as to the black squares, the mere fact of K2, QB2, and QR2 being unoccupied at this early stage, indicates that there must be various weak spots. These two defects ought certainly not to exist in the same Opening ; but if Black had the means of now speedily developing, there might be no great objection. But can he so develop? · Let us repeat the moves : 5 KtxP 5 P-QR3, 6 B-K2. Black is usually made to reply with 6 Kt-B3, which continuation, if maintained by play of a worrying nicety, may end in preserving Black from a ruinous inferiority. Whether so or not is, to our mind immaterial ; for we would not play the Sicilian upon such terms. And, moreover, we think that Black has a better line, viz., 6 Q-B2, which enables him to attempt operations of a freeing nature. There are also some grounds for supposing that this line may be adopted a move earlier, even though the results seem too eccentric to be favorable—e.g., 5 KtxP 5 Q-B2, 6 KKt-Kt5 6 Q-Ktsq, 7 B-K2 7 P-QR3, and we should imagine Black's game to be as good as in the normal grooves of the Sicilian. However, the QP always remains a source of anxiety, and we cannot have doubts respecting the future of this Defence."

In a subsequent issue of "Land and Water" Mr A Marriott writes :

"Will you allow me to supplement your very interesting article on the Sicilian Defence, by a variation which will, I think, confirm your opinion of its unsoundness, in regard to the continuation 6 Kt-B3. In a correspondence game played about a year ago, in which I played the attack, the following variation occurred : 1 P-K4 1 P-QB4, 2 Kt-QB3 2 Kt-QB3, 3 Kt-B3 3 P-K3, 4 P-Q4 4 PxP, 5 KtxP 5 P-QR3, 6 B-K2 6 Kt-B3, 7 KtxKt 7 KtPxKt, 8 P-K5 8 Kt-Q4, 9 Kt-K4 9 P-KB4. This seems the usual move at this juncture, and it is difficult to find anything more satisfactory, in view of White's threatened 10 P-QB4. I note from "Westminster Papers," in a game Zukertort v Anderssen, White replied to 9 P-KB4 with 10 B-R5ch 10 P-Kt3, 11 B-Kt5, and the game was eventually drawn. The continuation adopted by myself seems to firmly establish White's superiority : 10 PxP en pass 10 KtxP, 11 B-KKt5 11 Q-R4ch (if 11 B-K2, 12 BxKt 12 BxB, 13 Kt-Q6ch 13 K-K2, 14 Q-Q2 14 Q-B2, 15 R-Qsq), 12 B-Q2 12 Q-K4, 13 KtxKtch 13 QxKt, 14 B-QB3 14 P-K4, 15 B-Q3 15 B-Q3 (I cannot see a better move), 16 Castles, with a winning advantage. The move adopted by Mr Bird, 3 P-KKt3, appears to me to be the most favorable form of this hazardous Defence."

To this "Land and Water" replied :

"Your case stands established, we think. As to the combination of the Sicilian with the King's Fianchetto, to which you refer, it was adopted by Mr W N Potter in various games played by him in 1870-71, and it was about the same time he introduced his combination of the Centre Counter Gambit with the King's Fianchetto. As to the Sicilian, we do not think that Mr Bird adopted the King's Fianchetto in combination therewith until quite lately, while as to grafting the King's Fianchetto on the Centre Counter, it was, if we remember aright, adopted by Mr Blackburne in 1878 ; but we feel sure that he would unhesitatingly acknowledge that the combination in question had been introduced beforehand by Mr Potter. We may add that to each defence there is the same weakness, arising from the opponent playing B-K3, followed by Q-Q2, a line of attack established by Mr Blackburne, some time ago."

THE SICILIAN DEFENCE.

	1	2	3	4	5	6
	Vienna 1882 Congress.	London 1883 Congress.	London 1883 Congress.	Berlin 1881 Congress.	Vienna 1882 Congress.	Vienna 1882 Congress.
	Blackburne Mackenzie	Englisch Tschigorin	Blackburne Mortimer	Zukertort Schallopp	Blackburne Bird	Mason Paulsen
1	P-K4					
	P-QB4					
2	Kt-QB3				Kt-KB3	
	Kt-QB3		P-K3		P-K3	Kt-QB3
3	Kt-B3		Kt-B3		Kt-B3	P-Q4 (13)
	P-K3		Kt-QB3		Kt-QB3	PxP
4	P-Q4	B-K2 (4)	P-Q4		P-Q4	KtxP
	PxP	KKt-K2 (5)	PxP		PxP	Kt-B3
5	KtxP	P-Q4	KtxP		KtxP	KtxKt
	P-QR3	PxP	P-QR3 (9)	Kt-B3	P-QR3	KtPxKt
6	B-K2	KtxP	B-K2	KKt-Kt5	B-K2	B-Q3
	Kt-B3	Kt-Kt3 (6)	Kt-B3	B-Kt5	Kt-B3	P-Kt3
7	Castles	Castles	Castles	Kt-Q6ch	Castles	P-QKt3
	B-Kt5	B-K2	B-K2 (10)	K-K2 (A)	P-Q4	B-KKt2
8	KtxKt	B-K3	KtxKt	B-KB4	PxP	B-Kt2
	KtPxKt	Castles	KtPxKt	P-K4	KtxP	Castles
9	P-K5	P-B4	P-K5	Kt-B5ch	QKtxKt	Castles
	BxKt	B-B4? (7)	Kt-Q4	K-Bsq	PxKt	P-Q4
10	PxB	K-Rsq	Kt-K4	B-Q2	B-B3	PxP
	Kt-Q4	BxKt	P-KB4	P-Q3	B-K2	PxP
11	Q-Q4	BxB	Kt-Q6ch (11	Kt-Kt3	R-Ksq	Kt-Q2
	Castles	P-B4	BxKt	B-K3	Castles	B-Kt2
12	B-R3	B-B5	PxB	B-Q3	BxP!	Kt-B3
	R-Ksq	R-B2	Castles	P-KR4!	QxB	Q-B2
13	QR-Kt1 (1)	P-K5	P-QB4	Castles	KtxKt	B-K5
	P-KB4	P-Kt3	Kt-B3	Kt-KKt5	QxKt	Q-R4
14	R-Kt3!	B-K3	P-QKt3	P-KR3	RxB	Q-Ksq
	P-QR4	B-Kt2	B-Kt2	Q-R5	B-K3	QxQ
15	P-QB4	Kt-Kt5	P-B5	PxKt (B)	B-B4	KRxQ
	Kt-Kt5	R-Ktsq	P-QR4	PxP	KR-Qsq	P-K3
16	B-R5	Kt-Q6	R-Ksq	R-Ksq	Q-K2	Kt-Q4
	P-Kt3	R-KBsq	B-R3	Kt-Q5+	B-Q4 (12)	P-QR3
17	R-Kt3	KtxB	B-B3		R-B7	P-QKt4
	K-B2	RxKt	Q-Ktsq		Q-B3	Kt-Q2
18	Q-B4	B-B3	B-Kt2		Q-K5	BxB
	R-Rsq (2)	Q-K2	Q-Kt5		Q-QKt3	KxB
19	P-QB3	P-KKt3 (8)	R-QBsq		P-B4	P-KB4
	Q-Bsq	R-QB2	Q-KR5		B-B3	P-QR4
20	Q-Kt5	Q-Q2+	Q-Q2+		Q-KB5+	P-Kt5
	PxB (3)					P-R5 (14)

For Notes see page 68

NOTES, to page 67.

(1) Mr Sellman commends White's Opening highly.

(2) He dare not take the B, on account of Q-R6.

(3) Continued, 21 PxKt 21 K-Ksq, 22 P-Kt5 22 Q-B2, 23 Q-R6 (threatening to win the Q) 23 K-Qsq. 21 R-Kt7 24 Q-Ksq, 25 PxP 25 K-B2 (if PxP White mates in two), 26 Q-Q2 26 K-Qsq, 27 P-B7ch 27 KxP, 28 Q-Q6ch, and Black resigned.

(4) Mr Wayte says Dr Zukertort discovered that this is the right square for the B ; but the move is generally deferred until after 4 P-Q4 4 PxP, 5 KtxP.

(5) Kt-Q5 may be played here.

(6) Mr Wayte much prefers 6 P-KKt3, and 7 B-Kt2. Black would then have a good prospect of throwing forward P to Q4, and clearing his game.

(7) A lost move. P-Q3 should have been played.

(8) Confining the movements of the hostile Q. White keeps steadily in view the weak point at Q2.

(9) Formerly considered necessary, to prevent White from playing Kt-QKt5. It is, however, Mr Bird says, too slow for modern tactics, and experience has shown it to be no longer essential.

(10) P-Q4 should have been played here.

(11) Mr Bird says as a rule the effect of this check and establishment of either P or Kt at Q6 is very advantageous. It is so in the present instance.

(A) A line of defence invented by Chicago players.

(B) A slip. QKt-K2 would have given a safe game.

(12) The best resource was QR-B1.

(13) The old style of attack. It is usual now to develop both Knights before this advance.

(14) This was a stubbornly contested game of 67 moves. White won.

THE KING'S BISHOP'S OPENING.

By Mr W N Potter, in London "Land and Water."

THIS Opening is not in favor. Players of all strengths join in tabooing it. The 242 games of the London Tourney supply but one example of it. This fact, which speaks clearly enough as to the disesteem in which the Opening is held by first-rates, will probably be considered equally conclusive as to its merits. No deduction would be more erroneous. An interesting chapter could be written on the darkness of experts, and it could be studded with proofs from every great Tournament. These contests are, in fact, rubbish holes, into which moves and variations once thought to be correct are swept like so many dead leaves. As to the KB Opening, we are convinced that the majority of first-class players are profoundly ignorant of its real principles, and we will say the same of analysts. The cause of the mingled dislike and contempt with which it is regarded, may be found in the fact that it has been clothed with variations utterly alien from its real spirit. In our opinion, the KB Opening, far from being weak and inferior, is strong and reliable. We also consider that, properly handled, it yields just that enduring attack in which it has been said to be wanting. Our main notions will appear in the following variations. They will be found very brief and simple : 1 P-K4 1 P-K4, 2 B-B4 2 Kt-KB3, 3 Q-K2 3 Kt-B3, 4 P-QB3 4 B-B4, 5 Kt-B3 5 Castles, 6 P-Q3 6 P-Q4, 7 B-Kt3. This is our type position in this Opening, and we consider that whatever course Black now adopts, White retains such initiative superiority as ought to belong to him as first player

We will notice three natural replies. Firstly, 7 PxP, 8 PxP 8 B-K3, 9 Castles, or 9 B-B2, according to taste. Either course is good. Secondly, 7 B-K2, 8 Castles, or 8 B-B2, as in the last variation, for it is but a transposition. Thirdly, 7 B-KKt5, 8 Castles 8 PxP, 9 PxP 9 Kt-K2, 10 P-KR3, followed (if B-R4) by 11 B-Kt5, with the better game. Black would probably take the Kt, but Queen retakes, and White for choice.

Let us now go back : 1 P-K4 1 P-K4, 2 B-B4 2 B-B4, 3 Q-K2 3 Kt-QB3, 4 P-QB3 4 Kt-B3, 5 Kt-B3 5 Castles, 6 P-Q3 6 P-Q4, 7 B-Kt3, and the intelligent reader will see that we have again arrived at the type position. Herein lies our idea of this Opening. Sweeping away the Lopez Gambit, and a lot of other old rubbish, we confine the Opening to a simple and legitimate groove. Black may indeed diverge. He can play 5 P-Q3, to which we would still answer with 6 P-Q3, and White's game would be to our liking. It is true enough that 1 P-K4 1 P-K4, 2 Kt-KB3 2 Kt-QB3, 3 B-B4 3 B-B4, 4 P-B3 4 Kt-B3, 5 P-Q3 5 P-Q3, the well known Giuoco Piano variation of the Blackburne Zukertort match, could now be turned into our line, last above mentioned, by Q-K2, and we answer any objection on this score by saying that 6 Q-K2 would be our continuation in that branch of the Giuoco Piano. Altogether we hope to have made it clear that the KB Opening, simplified as above, is well worthy of being countenanced.

THE KING'S BISHOP'S GAMBIT. THE KING'S KNIGHT'S GAMBIT.

THOUGH theoretically the Defence obtains some advantage in these Openings, it is more the fashion to decline than to accept them in match play. Even the Muzio, in practical play, has a good recent record. In the Minor Tourney of the London Congress, 1883, Rev G A MacDonnell played the attack against Mr I Gunsberg, and won after a struggle of 66 moves. This was the only Muzio contested at that great gathering.

But little fresh analysis has appeared in these Openings, except in the King's Bishop's Gambit, to which we devote several pages.

KING'S BISHOP'S GAMBIT.

Game, Mortimer v Steinitz, London 1883 Congress.

	1		2		3		4		5
1	P-K4 / P-K4	2	P-KB4 / PxP	3	B-B4 / P-Q4	4	BxP / Q-R5ch	5	K-Bsq / P-KKt4
6	Kt-QB3 / B-Kt2	7	P-Q4 / Kt-K2	8	Kt-B3 / Q-R4	9	P-KR4 / P-KR3		

	1	2	3	4	5	6
10	P-K5? (1) / Castles		Q-Q3 (5) / P-K5	Castles	QKt-B3	
11	K-Ktsq / P-Kt5		Kt-Ksq / Kt-Kt3	Kt-K2 / KtxB	Kt-K2 / B-Kt5	Q-Kt3 (9)
12	Kt-Ksq / R-Qsq		Q-Kt5ch(6)	PxKt / P-KB4	P-B3 (8)	
13	Kt-Q3 (2) / Kt-Kt3	KtxB! (3)		B-Q2 (7)		
14		KtxKt / RxKt				
15		KtxP / QxKP†				
16		KtxR / QxKt+ (4)				

For Notes see opposite page.

NOTES, to opposite page.

(1) The "Handbuch" gives this move equal authority with 10 K-Ktsq. Mr Wayte says the move has been proved to be not feasible. Mr Steinitz says, in his notes to this game, that the advance of this P should be delayed as long as possible, in order to reserve Kt-K5 for some eventualities; and that the P at K4, also prevents the entrance of the Black Kt at KB4, which move often gives Black a strong counter attack.

(2) There is nothing better. If his KB moved Black could have taken the KP with B.

(3) The move made by Mr Steinitz was an error. He points out the correct play for Black in Col. 2.

(4) Black has two minor Pieces for the R, and a splendid position. The move Mr Steinitz made in the game (13 Kt-Kt3) led to a draw at the 63rd move.

(5) A move recently suggested by Mr W N Potter. Mr Wayte considers it important, and an improvement on 10 K-Ktsq for White.

(6) With a fine game, for Black must now move his K, with inconveniencies wherever it goes. Black might have played (the notes on White, 10 Q-Q3 are by Mr Potter) 11 P-QB3, whereupon 12 B-Kt3 12 Kt-Kt3, 13 Kt-K2, with an excellent game. Black could play 12 P-QKt3 but White gets a superiority by 13 Kt-K2 13 B-R3, 14 P-B4. We may remark that after 10 Q-Q3 10 P-Kt5, White could at once proceed with 11 Q-Kt5ch 11 K moves, 12 K-Ktsq, with what seems to be at least an even game. There is also 10 Q-Q3 10 P-Kt5, 11 Kt-Ksq 11 Kt-Kt3, 12 Kt-K2 and White for choice.

(7) With a fairly good game. However, 12 B-Kt5 would have been a better move for Black. White would then have had the choice of three replies, viz. 13 K-Ktsq, 13 K-B2 and 13 B-Q2, either of these moves preserving equality; but, as difficult play arises, we would, after 10 Q-Q3 10 Castles recommend 11 B-Kt3 as not only a simple but safe course, provided that it be followed up by Kt-K2, in almost every instance of play, other than obvious exceptions.

(8) Or B-Q2, or K-Ktsq, or K-B2, with a tenable game in either case, without prejudice to another twelfth move, viz.: QBxP, which has undoubted claims to be considered.

(9) There is a choice now of divers continuations at White's disposal, as for instance 12 P-R5, which is stronger here than in normal variations; 12 PxP, which has claims; 12 BxKtch, which is in accordance with latter day practice in analogous positions, though we must say that the moderns are prone to exchange for very slight reasons, and thereby they often rebel against the augmentation of force principle; 12 B-B4, which some would prefer, and it would apparently be a good sound move; 12 B-Kt3 which has points, though B-Kt5 might be a rather formidable reply; and 12 Q-Kt3, which seems to give White a kind of general control over the board, though this would be to a great extent neutralised by Black immediately Castling, after which there would be plenty of play on both sides. We shall be much surprised if it be not now admitted that 10 Q-Q3 has claims that are worthy of consideration,

KING'S BISHOP'S GAMBIT.

	7	8	9	10	11	12
	London 1883 Congress.	London 1883 Congress.	Toronto, 1881.		Match, Paris, 1883.	London 1884.
	Mortimer Bird	Mortimer Bird	Zukertort Ryall		Tschigorin De Rivière	Sutton Blackburne
1	P-K4 / P-K4					
2	P-KB4 / PxP					
3	B-B4 / Q-R5ch				P-Q4 (13)	Q-R5ch
4	K-Bsq / P-Q3 (1)				BxP / Q-R5ch	K-Bsq / P-KB4 (15)
5	Q-B3 (2) / Kt-QB3	Kt-KB3 / Q-R4			K-Bsq / P-KKt4	Kt-QB3(16) / Kt-KB3
6	P-KKt3 / Q-B3	P-KR4 (4) / Kt-KB3 (5)	P-Q4 / P-KKt4		Kt-KB3 / Q-R4	P-Q3 / P-KKt4
7	QxP / Kt-Q5	Kt-B3 / B-Kt5	Kt-B3 / B-K3	Kt-K2?	P-KR4 / P-KR3 (14)	Kt-B3 / Q-R4
8	B-Kt3 / B-K3	P-Q4 / Kt-B3	B-K2 / P-Kt5	P-KR4 / P-KB3	BxPch / QxB	P-KR4 / P-KR3
9	Kt-QB3 / P-KR4	B-Kt5 / Castles	Kt-Ksq / B-R3	P-K5 / B-Kt2	Kt-K5 / Q-B3	K-Ktsq / P-Kt5
10	P-Q3 / P-R5	BxKt / PxB	Kt-Q3 / P-B6	P-Q5 / BPxP	Q-R5ch / K-Qsq	Kt-K5 / R-R2
11	QxQ / KtxQ	BxP / P-Q4 (6)	PxP / Q-R6ch	Kt-Kt5 / K-Q2? (12)	Kt-B7ch / K-K2	Kt-K2 / PxP
12	K-Kt2 / BxB	Q-Q3 / BxKt! (7)	K-Ktsq (9) / PxP		KtxR / QxKt	BxP / Q-B4
13	BPxB / Kt-B7!	PxB / PxP	BxP / Kt-KB3		PxP / Q-K4	Q-KBsq / P-Q4
14	R-Ktsq / Kt-K8ch	PxP / RxP!	Q-Bsq / R-Ktsqch		PxP / QxQ	B-QKt3 / QKt-Q2
15	K-Bsq / PxP! (3)	QxR / Q-B6ch	B-Kt2 / BxB		RxQ / BxP	Kt-Kt3 / B-B4ch!
16	PxP / RxR+	Q-B2 (8) / QxRch	RxB / Kt-B3		Kt-B3 / B-K3	K-R2 / KtxKt
17		K-K2 / QxR+	Q-B2 (10) / KtxQP		P-Q3 / Kt-Q2	KtxQ / P-Kt6ch
18			Kt-B4 / Q-R3		R-R4 / R-KBsq	BxP (17) / QKt-Kt5ch
19			R-KBsq / B-B5		Kt-K2 / Kt-K4	K-R3 / Kt-K6
20			R-Ksq / KtxBP+(11		Kt-Q4+	Q-B4 / BxKtch(18)

For Notes see opposite page.

NOTES, to opposite page.

(1) Mr Bird says: "I adopted this move with much success in America in 1877. Although it is not recommended in the works of any of the leading authorities on the Openings, it has stood the test of practice well, and I believe is better than P-KKt4, the move usually played in the magnificent games of Anderssen, Harrwitz, Lowenthal, Kieseritzky, and other great masters who were most partial to the unrivalled 'Bishop's Gambit Opening.'"

(2) Mr Bird continues: "Kt-QB3 is justly considered the best move at this point, as it threatens at once to go to Q5, a formidable square. Kt-KB3, or P-Q4, are also frequently played, the order of them being varied. The move in the text (Q-KB3) has the sanction of Staunton, and has been regarded as free from objection by other leading authorities. With due respect, however, I do not regard it as perfectly satisfactory. The 'Bishop's Gambit' is rarely ventured in Tournaments or great games, being an Opening of a dangerous and decisive character. Out of the 283 games in the Vienna Tournament of 1882 there was only one example of it."

(3) Threatening P-Kt7.

(4) Mr Bird's notes: "I do not recollect to have observed this move at this point before in an important contest; it appears, moreover, worthy of attention, and, I think, strong; it compels Black to play P-KKt4 at once, if he intends to attempt to keep the Gambit Pawn, and this deprives him of a numerous choice of moves which he might otherwise select."

(5) Black preferred not to attempt to maintain the Gambit Pawn.

(6) Mr Bird doubts the prudence of this move, which appears to lose important time.

(7) The Kt could not be allowed to go to K5.

(8) Black calculated on White playing to Ktsq, losing the B and not the R; Black would then have obtained an equivalent in position, for the sacrifice of a R for B and P.

(9) Dr Ryall says K-B2 is probably better.

(10) P-Q5 would be bad.

(11) Dr Ryall won on the 42nd move.

(12) Dr Ryall knows of two instances where this absurd move was made.

(13) A favorite defence of Morphy, who continued, however, 4 Kt-KB3.

(14) A grave error. B-Kt2 is the only correct move.

(15) A risky counter Gambit, not to be commended.

(16) P-K5 would be better. By the move in the text White goes on the defensive.

(17) If KtxP Black mates in four.

(18) Continued: 21 K-R2 21 QKt-Kt5ch, 22 K-R3 22 Kt-B7ch, 23 K-R2 23 KKt-Kt5ch, 24 K-Ktsq 24 KtxPch, 25 K-Bsq 25 KtxQ, 26 BxKt 26 Castles, and White resigned.

DEFEAT OF GRIMM'S ATTACK IN THE KING'S BISHOP'S GAMBIT.

THE following analysis, from Mr A G Sellman, of Baltimore, first appeared in "Brentano's Chess Monthly," August 1881.

WHITE.	BLACK.	WHITE.	BLACK.
1 P-K4	1 P-K4	12 KtxKP	12 Q-B4
2 P-KB4	2 PxP	13 Q-R5	13 BxKt
3 B-B4	3 Q-R5ch	14 PxB	14 P-QB3
4 K-Bsq	4 P-KKt4	15 B-Q2	15 PxKt
5 Kt-KB3	5 Q-R4	16 BxQP	16 Kt-QB3
6 P-Q4	6 B-Kt2	17 PxP	17 B-K3
7 Kt-B3	7 P-Q3	18 BxB	18 PxB
8 P-K5	8 PxP	19 R-KBsq	19 QxBP
9 P-KR4	9 P-KR3	20 BxP	20 Q-QB4ch
10 Kt-Q5	10 K-Qsq	21 K-R2	21 KtxP
11 K-Ktsq	11 Q-Kt3	22 P-Kt6	

and the "books" dismiss the game, asserting that White must win. Suppose, however, Black continues with 22 Kt-KB3, then we think we can prove, by the following variations, that the reverse will happen.

Firstly :

	22 Kt-KB3
23 B-Kt5	23 QKt-Kt5ch
24 K-Kt3	

(if 24 QxKt 24 PxBch wins. If 24 K-R3 24 QxB wins.)

	24 Q-K4ch
25 K-B3	25 PxB
26 QxRch	26 K-B2
27 Q-Kt7ch	27 K-Kt3

and Black wins easily. White must sacrifice his Queen to delay the impending mate over four moves.

Secondly :

	22 Kt-KB3
23 P-Kt7	23 R-KKtsq
24 B-Kt5	

(if 24 Q-R4 24 Kt-Kt5ch, 25 K-R3 25 RxP, 26 BxP 26 R-Kt3, and Black ought to win. If 24 R or Q-Qsqch, Black can reply with 24 K-K2, in either case getting a safe game, and still retaining the advantage of a Piece.)

	24 PxB
25 RxKt	25 Kt-Kt5ch
26 QxKt	26 Q-K4ch
27 K-R3	27 QxR
28 R-Qsqch	28 K-K2

29 Q-Kt4ch   29 K-B2
and wins.

Thirdly :

White might play for his twenty-third move QxKt or BxKt, but, in either case, Black speedily wins. In the first place :

	22 Kt-KB3
23 QxKt	23 Kt-Kt5ch, &c.

In the second place :

	22 Kt-KB3
23 BxKt	23 KtxQ
24 BxR	24 Q-Q3ch
25 K-Ktsq	25 Kt-Kt6
26 R-B7	

(if 26 P-Kt7 26 K-B2 wins.)

	26 Q-Q8ch
27 K-R2, or B2	

and Black wins easily.

Fourthly :

	22 Kt-KB3
23 Q or R-Qsqch	23 K-K2

and Black still holds his advantage in force, with a perfectly safe game.

ALLGAIER-THOROLD.

	1	2	3	4	5
1	P-K4 / P-K4	2 P-KB4 / PxP	3 Kt-KB3 / P-KKt4	4 P-KR4 / P-Kt5	5 Kt-Kt5 / P-KR3

	1	2	3	4	5	6
	Chicago, 1884.	Team match, London, 1884.	Glasgow, 1884.	St Paul, Minn, 1884.	London, 1881.	Leamington, 1881.
	Adair Zukertort	Thorold Ballard	Wright Spens	Hamilton Rohrer	Gunsberg Ballard	Coker Aspa
6	KtxP / KxKt					
7	P-Q4 / P-Q4				P-Q3 (14)	
8	BxP / PxP (1)				B-B4ch / K-Kt3	BxP / B-K2
9	B-B4ch / K-Kt3 (2)	K-Kt2			BxP / Kt-KB3	B-B4ch / K-Kt2
10	Castles (3) / B-Kt2	Castles (A) / Kt-KB3		B-K5ch / Kt-KB3	Q-Q3 (15) / Q-Ksq	Castles / Kt-KB3
11	P-B3 / Kt-K2 (4)	Kt-B3 / B-K2	R-R2	Castles / B-K2	Kt-B3 / Kt-B3	Kt-B3 / R-Ksq (17)
12	Kt-Q2 / B-B4	B-K5 / Kt-B3	Q-Q2 / Kt-B3	Kt-B3 / Kt-B3	P-R5ch / KtxRP	P-K5 / PxP
13	B-K3 (5) / R-Bsq	P-R5 / KtxB	QR-Qsq / KtxP	R-B4 / KtxB	RxKt / Kt-Kt5	BxP / Kt-B3
14	KtxP! / K-R2 (6)	PxKt / B-B4ch(10)	KtxP / Kt-B6ch	PxKt / QxQch	Q-K2 / KxR	Q-Ksq / KtxB
15	Kt-Kt3 / K-Rsq (7)	K-Rsq / KtxP (11)	PxKt / QxQ	RxQ / B-QB4ch	P-R3 / Kt-B3	QxKt / Q-Q3
16	Q-Q2 / Q-Q3	R-B7ch / K-Kt3	BxQ / KtxKt	K-R2 / Kt-R4	Castles / K-Kt3	Q-K3 / P-B3 (18)
17	B-B4 / Q-QKt3 (8)	QxQ (12) / RxQ	PxKt / B-QB4ch	R-B7ch / K-Kt3	Kt-Q5! / R-R2 (16)	Kt-K4! / KtxKt
18	QR-Ksq / QKt-B3 (9)	RxP / B-Kt3	K-Kt2 / B-Q2	RxP / P-Kt6ch	P-K5 / R-B2	R-B7ch / K-Rsq
19	BxRP / B-Kt3	B-B7ch / K-Kt2	B-B3ch / K-Kt3	K-Rsq / B-Kt3	B-Q3ch / K-Kt2	QxKt / Q-R7ch
20	BxBch / KxB	RxB / KxB	R-B6ch / K-R4	R-Q6ch / K-B4	Kt-B6+	K-Bsq / Q-R8ch(19)
21	Q-Kt5 / RxRch	RxQR / RxR	QR-Bsq! / KxP	R-B7ch / K-Kt5		K-K2 / B-KB4
22	RxR+	KtxP / K-K3	B-Q2 / P-Kt6	R-Kt6 / KxP		RxQB / B-Q3
23		R-Ksq / P-Kt6 (13)	R-Rsqch+	KtxP / B-Kt5+		R-K5 / RxR (20)

For Notes see page 76.

NOTES, to page 75.

(1) Rev C E Ranken says, in the following notes to this game, that this move, it is true, breaks White's centre, but then it lets in his KB, and isolates the Pawn. We therefore prefer either P-B6 for Black's 7th move, or to bring the KKt here to B3, for then if the P attacked the Kt. it would go to R4, and, if 9 B-K5, Black could answer with Kt-QB3.

(2) Dr Zukertort, we believe, holds that this, followed by B-Kt2, is best.

(3) There would be no advantage now or at the next move in P-R5ch, as the K would simply retire to R2.

(4) Kt-KB3 is certainly stonger, defending both the weak Pawns, as will be seen anon.

(5) Preparing an ingenious attack, the point of which seems to have escaped Black's observation, or he would have replied with Q-Q2, or K-R2.

(6) Mr Ranken agrees with "The Field," in its notes on this game, that Black had ample time now to play QKt-B3, though at the sacrifice of the KKtP, e.g., 14 QKt-B3, 15 Kt-Kt3 15 K-R2, 16 KtxB 16 KtxKt, 17 B-Q3 17 Kt-K2, 18 QxP 18 Q-Q2, 19 R-B3 19 K-Rsq, &c.

(7) This does not turn out well at all. QKt-B3 would still be better.

(8) The Q should have gone to KKt3, and. if the P attack her, to R2, for now she is speedily shut out from the game.

(9) If 18 Kt-Ktsq, then 19 KtxB 19 RxKt, 20 R-K8 20 R-Bsq, 21 RxR 21 BxR, 22 B-K5ch 22 B-Kt2, 23 R-B8, and wins.

(10) "The Glasgow Herald" thinks that this move, followed by the capture of the RP, gives Black a winning game.

(11) This move anticipates the threatened check at B7.

(12) Necessary, on account of the check at R5.

(13) Continued, 24 P-B4 24 B-Q5, 25 Kt-Q2 25 R-KBsq, 26 Kt-B3 26 B-B7, 27 R-Qsq 27 RxKt. followed by 28 Kt-B5, and Black wins.

(14) Mr. Potter calls this a very ineffective move. The proper move is P-Q4 or P-B6.

(15) Mr. Potter says Kt-B3 is decidedly better.

(16) He would prefer B-Kt2 here, as Black cannot escape some loss now.

(17) Kt-R4 would have been better, compelling the QB to retreat.

(18) Weak. B-Bsq was best.

(19) B-KB4 was the only resource.

(20) Continued, 24 PxR 24 QxR (hoping for the draw if White capture the B), 25 B-Q3! 25 K-Ktsq, 26 Q-R7ch 26 K-Bsq, 27 QxRPch 27 K-K2, 28 QxBch 28 K-B2, 29 B-Kt6ch 29 K-Kt2, and White mates in three.

(a) Mr Potter says 10 Q-Q2 has some claims here, but he does not regard it as trustworthy. But there is another continuation, to wit, 10 Q-K2. Upon this eccentric and apparently aimless move he bases his hope "that the brilliant career of the Allgaier-Thorold shall not for a long time come to a close." Black has three noticeable replies, namely, QxQP, Kt-QB3 and Kt-KB3. In answer to the first, White proceeds 11 P-B3 11 Q-B4, 12 B-K3, followed by B-Q4ch, and afterward R-KBsq, or Kt-Q3, or Castles, as the case may require. 11 P-B3 11 Q-Qsq, 12 B-K5ch 12 Kt interposes, 13 R-Bsq 13 B-K2, 14 Kt-Q2 14 Kt-B3, 15 BxKtch 15 BxB, 16 Castles, with a strong attack. If Black 11 Q-Kt3, 12 B-K5 12 Kt interposes, 13 R-Bsq, with a tolerable game. White may also play 11 B-K3, with a strong game. It is to be noted that 10 Q-K2 10 QxP, frequently allows White to Castle. Mr Potter promises to deal with Black's other defences at his tenth move, at some future time.

SALVIO. **ALLGAIER-KIESERITZSKY.**

$$1\ \frac{\text{P-K4}}{\text{P-K4}} \qquad 2\ \frac{\text{P-KB4}}{\text{PxP}} \qquad 3\ \frac{\text{Kt-KB3}}{\text{P-KKt4}}$$

	1	2	3	4	1	2
	Vienna 1882 Congress.	Weisbaden 1880 Con.	Coml Gaz Cor Tourney 1883.	Berlin 1881 Congress.	Vienna 1882 Congress.	New York, 1884
	Steinitz Tschigorin	Consultation Game	Kittson Tatnall	Tschigorin Winawer	Steinitz Zukertort	Thornton Steinitz
4	B-B4 / P-Kt5				P-KR4 / P-Kt5	
5	Kt-K5 / Q-R5ch				Kt-K5 / Kt-KB3(13)	B-Kt2
6	K-Bsq / Kt-KR3				B-B4 / P-Q4	P-Q4 / Kt-KB3
7	P-Q4 / P-B6			P-B6 (11) /	PxP / B-Kt2	B-B4 / P-Q4
8	Kt-B3 / Kt-B3 (1)	B-B4 (4) / P-Q3	P-Kt3 / Q-R6ch	Kt-B3 / PxPch	Kt-QB3 / Castles	PxP / Castles
9	B-B4 / P-Q3	Kt-Q3 / PxPch	K-B2 / Q-Kt7ch	KxP / Q-R6ch	P-Q4 / Kt-R4	BxP / KtxP
10	KtxKt / PxPch	KxP / Kt-B3	K-K3 / P-KB4	K-Ktsq / P-Q4 (12)	Kt-K2 / P-QB4 (14)	B-KKt3 / Kt-K6
11	KxP / PxKt	B-KKt3 / Q-K2 (5)	Kt-B3 / P-B3	BxP / KtxB	P-B3 / PxP	Q-K2! / QxQP
12	R-KBsq / B-Q2	Kt-B2 / B-Kt2	Kt-Q3 (8) / PxP	KtxKt / B-Q3	PxP / Kt-Q2 (15)	P-B3 / Q-Kt3
13	Q-Q2 / B-Kt2	P-B3 / B-Q2	Kt-B4 / Kt-B4ch	Q-Ksq / Kt-Q2	KtxKt (16) / BxKt	B-Kt3 / B-K3
14	QR-Ksq / CastlesKR	Kt-Q2 / CastlesQR	KxP / P-Q4ch	KtxKt / BxKt	Q-Q3 / R-Bsq	Kt-Q2 / Kt-B3
15	R-K3 / K-Rsq	P-Kt4 (6) / P-B4	BxP / PxBch	P-K5 / CastlesQR	KtxP / R-Ksqch	KtxKt / BxB
16	Kt-K2 / P-Q4 (2)	P-Kt5 / Kt-R4	QKtxP / Kt-Q3ch	PxB! / QR-Ksq	K-Qsq / P-Kt4	Kt-K7ch! / K-Rsq
17	PxP / Kt-B4	R-Ksq (7) / KtxB	K-Q3 / Q-B7 (9)	Q-R5+	KtxKt / PxB	PxB / KR-Ksq
18	R-Q3 / Q-R4	KtxKt / BxKtP	B-K3 / B-B4ch		Q-QR3 / BxP	Kt-B4 / KtxKt
19	K-Ktsq / Kt-R5	PxP / Q-B2	K-B3 / Kt-Kt4ch		B-Q2 / Q-Kt3	PxKt / B-B3
20	Kt-Kt3 / Q-Kt3	Kt-K3 / KtxP	K-Kt3 / BxPch		B-B3 / R-K6	CastlesQR / RxKt
21	Q-R5 / Kt-B6ch	KtxKt / QxKt	QxB / QxBch		R-Ksq / BxB	QxP / B-Kt2
22	K-Rsq / P-R4 (3)	QxP / QxQ+	KtxQ / KtxPch(10)		RxR / QxR (17)	KR-Bsq / Q-Kt6 (18)

For Notes see page 78.

K

NOTES, to page 77.

(1) P-Q3, followed on Kt retreating to Q3 by PxPch, is considered best.

(2) An unwarranted sacrifice, though leading to some lively play.

(3) Continued, 23 P-Q6 23 P-KB4, 24 QxQBP 24 QR-Qsq, 25 R-K3 25 P-R5, 26 Kt-K2 26 Ktx QP, 27 R-K7 27 KtxKt, 28 BxKt 28 P-Kt6, 29 B-B3 29 R-KKtsq, 30 PxP 30 PxP, 31 K-Kt2! 31 B-R3, 32 B-K5ch, and Black resigned.

(4) This game was contested between Bird, Blackburne, and Winawer (White), and L Paulsen, W Paulsen, and Zukertort (Black).

(5) Avoiding the lock-up of the Q following Q-R6ch.

(6) Mr Steinitz pronounces this move both premature and hazardous.

(7) Mr Reichhelm says this move loses the game, as it allows the exchange of the B for Kt. Black won on the 47th move.

(8) The object of this deviation from the usual book move, B-Q3, is to imprison the Black Q, but the result condemns the strategy.

(9) A lost move, as White does not check and capture R.

(10) Continued, 23 K-B3 23 KtxQ, 24 KxKt 24 P-KR4, 25 Kt(K3)-Q5 25 Kt-R3? (the losing move. B-Q3 was the proper move), 26 QR-Ksqch 26 K-B2, 27 R-K5+.

(11) The Cochrane variation, which Steinitz played successfully against Anderssen and Zukertort.

(12) P-Q3 is better play.

(13) Mr Steinitz says this can be played in lieu of Paulsen's B-Kt2, the moves being merely transposed.

(14) This attempt to break through with the P, Mr Steinitz says, is not new, but in this game Dr Zukertort has hit upon the exact point to apply it.

(15) An excellent move, giving Black the advantage in all variations.

(16) If KtxKtP the reply Kt-Kt3 wins a Piece.

(17) Continued, 23 PxB 23 Q-Kt8ch, 24 K-Q2 24 QxPch, 25 K-K3 25 R-Ksqch, 26 K-Q4 26 Q-K5 ch, 27 K-B5 27 Q-K2ch, 28 P-Q6 28 Q-K4ch, 29 KxP 29 Q-K5ch, 30 K-Kt3 30 R-Ktsqch, 31 Q-Kt4, 31 RxQch, 32 PxR 32 Q-Q6ch, 33 K-Kt2 33 Q-Q5ch, and White resigned.

(18) Continued, 23 R-B2 23 R-KBsq, 24 R-Q3 24 R-K3?, 25 RxP! 25 RxR, 26 QxR 26 R-B8ch 27 B-Ksq 27 Q-Kt3, 28 QxQ 28 RPxQ, 29 K-Q2 29 K-Ktsq, 30 R-Q8ch 30 B-Bsq, 31 R-Q7? (giving Black a chance to draw. White's correct move was 31 K-K2) 31 B-Q3!, 32 K-K2 32 R-Kt8!, 33 K-B2 33 R-R8, 34 K-K2 34 R-Kt8, and the game was drawn.

	KING'S GAMBIT			KING'S GAMBIT DECLINED		
	1	2	3	1	2	3
	London 1883 Congress. Tschigorin Sellman	London 1883 Congress. Mortimer Rosenthal	London 1883 Minor Tour. Ensor V.Bardeleben			Philadelphia 1882. Steinitz Barbour
1	P-K4 / P-K4			P-K4 / P-K4		
2	P-KB4 / PxP			P-KB4 / B-B4 (10)		Kt-KB3
3	Kt-KB3 / P-KKt4		P-Q4 (5) / Q-R5ch	Kt-KB3 / P-Q3		PxP / KtxP
4	B-B4 / B-Kt2	P-KR4 / P-Kt5	K-K2 / P-Q4	B-B4 / Kt-KB3		Kt-KB3 / Kt-Kt4 (14)
5	P-Q4 / P-Kt5?	Kt-K5 / P-Q3 (3)	PxP / B-Q3 (6)	P-B3 / Q-K2! (11)		P-B3 / P-Q4
6	Kt-Ktsq (1) / Q-R5ch	KtxKtP / B-K2	P-B4 / P-QKt3	Q-K2! / P-B3!	Kt-B3?	PxPenpass / BxP
7	K-Bsq / Kt-QB3	P-Q4 / BxPch	Kt-KB3 / B-KKt5	P-Q3 / P-QKt4	P-QR4 (12) / P-QR4	P-Q4 / Q-K2ch
8	P-B3 / B-R3	Kt-B2 / Q-Kt4	K-Q2 / BxKt	B-Kt3 / KKt-Q2	P-B5 / Kt-KKt5	K-B2 / Kt-K5ch
9	Kt-QR3 / P-R3?	Kt-B3 / Kt-KB3	QxB / Kt-Q2	P-B5 — / B-Kt2—	P-Q4 (13) / PxP	K-Ktsq / Castles
10	P-KKt3 / PxP	Q-B3 / Kt-Kt5	P-QR3 / P-QR4		PxP / BxP	B-Q3 / P-KB4
11	K-Kt2 / BxB	Kt-Qsq / KtxKt	Kt-B3 / Kt-K2		KtxB / KtxKt	P-B4 / P-B4!
12	QxB / PxP	KtxKt / Kt-B3	K-B2 / CastlesKR		QxKt / Kt-B7ch	P-Q5 / Kt-Q2
13	RxP / Q-K2	P-B3 / B-Kt6	B-Q3 / Kt-Kt3		K-Qsq / KtxR	Q-K2 / Kt-K4 (15)
14	Q-B4 / P-Q3	B-K2 / B-Q2	B-Q2 / Q-B3		QxP / R-Bsq	KtxKt / BxKt
15	R-KBsq / Kt-Qsq	B-Q2 / CastlesQR	Kt-K4! / QxP		B-KR6 / B-Q2	P-KKt3 / B-Q5ch
16	R-R5 / P-Kt4?	CastlesQR / P-B4	B-B3 / Q-K6		QxRch / QxQ	K-Kt2 / R-Ksq
17	B-Kt3 / Kt-K3	PxP / QxP	QxQ (7) / PxQ		BxQ+	R-Ksq / B-Q2
18	Q-K3 / P-R3	R-R5 / Q-B2	QR-Ksq (8) / B-B5			Kt-Q2 / Q-B3
19	Kt-B2 / Kt-Kt4	P-Kt3 / QR-Bsq	P-KKt3 / B-R3			KtxKt / PxKt
20	B-Q5 / R-Ktsq (2)	R-Rsq / Kt-K2 (4)	B-Q4 / QR-Ksq (9)			BxP / B-B4 (16)

For Notes see page 80.

NOTES, to page 79.

(1) Dr Zukertort says White may enter here into the Muzio with **6 Castles or 6 BxP**, or proceed with Kt-K5.   The text move is new, but perfectly safe.

(2) Continued, 21 Kt-Kt4 21 Kt-B3?, 22 **QxKt** 22 KtxB (if PxQ, White's reply is RxRch+), 23 QxKt+.

(3) Mr Minchin says it is singular that such a master of the Openings as M. Rosenthal should have selected this old fashioned form of defence, when that springing from Kt-KB3, and B-Kt2 gives so decided an advantage, that the attack is now rarely ventured on.

(4) Through errors White lost this game at move 53.

(5) An old move—the Polerio Gambit.

(6) As at the similar stage of the Steinitz Gambit, Black may here play 5 Q-K2ch, giving White the choice between a very inferior game and a draw by perpetual check.   As Black is playing to win in this game, Mr W M Gattie would prefer the following continuation for Black, 5 B-KKt5ch, 6 Kt-B3 6 Kt-Q2, 7 P-B4 7 Castles, 8 K-Q2 8 Kt-B3, with a good game.

(7) Q-R5 would have been a difficult move for Black to meet.

(8) An error.   White should have played **KtxB**, afterwards regaining the P by QR-Ksq and B-Q4.

(9) Further errors enabled Black to win on the 46th move.

(10) Mr Max Judd says this is Black's best reply.   In his opinion, the capture of the Pawn, whatever it may be theoretically, **more** often leads to defeat than success in practice and even in match play.   Taking the P gives the **first** player many ways of instituting a strong attack.   Odds givers are very partial to the Gambit accepted.   By declining the Gambit with 2 B-B4 the game remains even.

(11) Mr Judd says this is the **best** move at this stage, and leads in many cases to decided advantage for Black.   It **prevents** the establishment of White's centre Pawns.   In this line of play Black must not **exchange** his QB for the White KKt.   The books advise it, but Mr Judd says it is not the best play.

(12) Preventing Black from **exchanging** QKt for B, and having other obvious intentions.

(13) White might also play R-Bsq.

(14) An invention by Mr Barbour.

(15) Showing the purpose of his 11th move.

(16) Continued, 21 Q-B3 21 RxB, and Mr Steinitz resigned, seeing that if he took the R **he** would lose his Q by B-R6ch, forcing the K to abandon the defence of the Q.

IRREGULAR OPENINGS.

THE popularity of the Irregular Openings in the recent Chess Congresses has already been referred to. Specimens of these efforts to avoid book play are very frequent in the Book of the London Chess Congress, 1883, and indeed the volume might serve as a modern treatise on the subject. In the 242 games the first player opened 182 times with P-K4, and otherwise 60 times. The second player replied to 1 P-K4 with the same move 110 times, and otherwise 72 times. White played 1 P-KB4 eight times; 1 Kt-QB3 once; 1 P-Q4 twenty-four times; 1 Kt-KB3 nine times; 1 P-K3 twice; and 1 P-QB4 sixteen times. Ten of the thirty-two games contested at that meeting by Dr Zukertort had irregular Openings. We present one page from the London games, as examples of prevailing ideas in declining to offer any of the standard debuts.

Mr E Freeborough says the Opening 1 P-KB4, advocated by Mr Bird, does not stop the reply from Black 1 P-K4, if the latter wishes to play From's Gambit.

IRREGULAR OPENINGS.

	1	2	3	4	5	6
	London 1883 Congress.	London 1883 Congress.	London 1883 Congress.	London 1883 Congress.	London 1883 Congress.	London 1883 Congress.
	Zukertort Rosenthal	Zukertort Englisch	Zukertort Mason	Zukertort Winawer	Mason Steinitz	Tschigorin Blackburne
1	Kt-KB3 / P-Q4			P-Q4 / P-Q4		P-KB4 / P-K3
2	P-Q4 / P-K3		Kt-KB3 /	P-K3 / B-B4	B-B4 / P-QB4 (18)	P-K3 / P-QKt3
3	P-K3 / Kt-KB3	/ P-QB4	P-K3 / B-Kt5	Kt-KB3 / P-K3	PxP? / Kt-QB3	Kt-KB3 / B-Kt2
4	P-B4 / B-K2	B-K2 (4) / Kt-KB3	B-K2 / BxKt	B-K2 / B-Q3	Kt-KB3 / P-B3 (19)	P-QKt3 / B-K2
5	Kt-B3 / Castles	Castles / Kt-B3	BxB / P-K3	Castles / Kt-KB3	P-K3 / P-K4	B-Kt2 / B-B3
6	B-K2 / P-B4	P-QKt3 / B-K2	Castles / B-Q3	P-B4 / P-B3	B-Kt3 / BxP	Kt-B3 / Kt-K2
7	Castles / Kt-B3	B-Kt2 / Castles	P-B4 / P-B3	Kt-B3 / QKt-Q2	P-B3 / KKt-K2	B-Q3 (22) / Kt-Q4
8	P-QKt3 / Kt-K5?	P-B4 / BPxP?	Kt-B3 / QKt-Q2	P-B5 / B-B2	QKt-Q2 / B-Kt3	Q-K2 / Kt-B3
9	B-Kt2 / BPxP?	KPxP / P-QKt3	P-QKt3 / R-QBsq	P-QKt4 / P-QR3?	B-K2 / Castles (20)	P-QR3 / KtxKt
10	KtxKt! / PxKt	QKt-Q2 (5) / B-Kt2	B-Q2 (10) / B-Ktsq (11)	P-QR4 / Kt-Kt5 (15)	Castles / Kt-B4	PxKt / P-K4
11	KtxP / P-B3 (1)	R-Bsq / R-Bsq	R-Ksq (12) / P-KR4	P-KR3 / P-KR4	P-K4 / KtxB	CastlesQR / Q-K2
12	KtxKt / PxKt	B-Q3 / B-R3 (6)	PxP / BPxP	B-Kt2 (16) / B-K5	RPxKt / P-Q5	B-B5 / CastlesQR
13	Q-B2 / P-KB4	R-Ksq (7) / Kt-QR4 (8)	P-K4 / PxP	P-Kt5 / BxKt	PxP / PxP	KR-Ksq / KR-Ksq
14	P-B5 (2) / Q-B2	Q-K2 / B-Kt5	KtxP / KtxKt	BxB / Q-Kt4	B-B4ch / K-Rsq	Q-B2 / P-Kt3
15	P-QKt4 / R-Ktsq	P-QR3 / B-Q3 (9)	BxKt / Kt-B3	P-Kt6! / B-Qsq	Kt-Kt3 / B-Kt5	B-R3 / B-Kt2
16	B-QB3 / B-B3	P-B5! / BxB	BxP / BxPch	PxKt / PxP	B-Q5 / Kt-K4!	B-Q5 / P-Kt3
17	QR-Qsq / B-Q2	QxB / B-B5	K-Bsq / R-QKtsq	BxP / P-B4!	BxP / R-QKtsq	P-K4 / PxKP
18	BxB / RxB	R-B2 / Kt-B3	Q-B3 / B-Q3	P-B4! / QxB	B-Q5 / P-B4!	RxP / Q-Bsq
19	R-Q6! / RxP (3)	P-QKt4 / B-Ktsq	B-Kt5 / B-K2 (13)	QxQ / PxQ	QKt-Q2 (21) / P-B5	R-K2 / PxP
20	Q-Q2+ /	P-Kt5+ /	QR-Qsq / Castles (14)	P-K4 / B-B3 (17)	Q-R4 / KtxKtch+	RxR / QxR (23)

(1) Dr Zukertort says M Rosenthal plays this game below his usual standard. He has already a bad game, and the text move loses time on the K side, and gives White an opportunity to break up the Q side.

(2) Blocking the action of both hostile Bishops, and opening a good square for his B at QB4.

(3) A blunder, but Black's game is lost, his position being blocked and his Pawns weak.

(4) Dr Zukertort says White may also proceed with 4 P-QKt3, 5 B-Kt2, and 6 B-Q3.

(5) After the exchange of Pawns on the previous move White makes the text move to protect the QBP, and keep the QB file clear for the Rooks.

(6) Black errs here in attacking White's QBP, which is not open to assault.

(7) Threatening to win a Pawn with 14 PxP 14 BxB, 15 PxKt 15 B-Kt4, 16 Kt-K5 16 Q-Ksq.

(8) PxP would be better.

(9) Overlooking White's next move. He should have captured the Kt.

(10) White could not play the KP on account of Black's reply B-Kt5

(11) Preparing to attack on the K side.

(12) Making an outlet for the K, and preparing to attack in the centre.

(13) If 19 Kt-Kt5 White wins a Piece by RxPch, &c.

(14) White won after a hard battle of 58 moves.

(15) A premature attack.

(16) Dr Zukertort says that he should have played B-Q2.

(17) This game was a prolonged struggle of 79 moves. Black overlooked a draw at move 45, and again at move 50. White finally won.

(18) Mr Steinitz says this is a novelty which seems to break the force of this attack, once so much dreaded that Morphy avoided it against Harrwitz by 1 P-KB4, after losing twice with the defence 1 P-Q4.

(19) Securing a centre, and an excellent game.

(20) Kt-B4 would have been premature, on account of the reply Kt-R4.

(21) White probable saw too late that he could not capture the QP. 19 QKtxP 19 PxP, 20 BxP 20 KBxKt, and White cannot retake without losing his Q.

(22) Mr Bird says White has unquestionably the better Opening.

(23) This was a fine game of 45 moves, and was won by White.

THE BLACKMAR GAMBITS.

THE following account and analyses of these methods of commencing the Game have been re-arranged, and in a few instances slight revisions have been made, by Mr Edward Marks, of the Athenæum Chess Club, London ; who, however, disclaims any responsibility for the accuracy of the analyses.

The American Supplement introduces the Blackmar Gambits as follows :—

" Mr A E Blackmar, of New Orleans, sends to the editor the following analysis of winning positions in two interesting Gambits invented by him, and which he has been playing for four years. The second Gambit is not played much, because few make use of the Hollandish Defence, Black 1 P-KB4.

" In the first Gambit the general opinion is that Black should not capture the second Pawn, but play 3 P-K3 or 3 P-K4, as suggested by Mr Chas. A Maurian.

" Mr Blackmar has a manuscript book of over 300 games played at the Gambits, and his conclusion is that both lead to most interesting positions, giving White an immense variety of brilliant attacks to repay for the Pawn sacrificed.

" The second Gambit resembles From's Gambit at White's fourth move, except that White is a move ahead."

FIRST GAMBIT (see pages 85-88) :—

$$1 \frac{\text{P-Q4}}{\text{P-Q4}} \quad 2 \frac{\text{P-K4}}{\text{PxP}} \quad 3 \frac{\text{P-KB3}}{\text{PxP}} \quad 4 \frac{\text{KtxP}}{}$$

Position after White's 4th move.
BLACK.

WHITE.

SECOND GAMBIT (see page 89) :—

THE BLACKMAR GAMBIT.

(See Diagram on page 84.)

	1	2	3	4	5	6
4	B-B4					
5	P-B3 / P-K3					
6	B-QB4 / B-K2					B-K2 / P-K4
7	Castles / Kt-KB3					KtxP / BxKt
8	QKt-Q2 / P-B3					RxB / Q-R5ch
9	Kt-K5 (1) / B-Kt3			Castles	Kt-Kt5 / Castles	P-KKt3 / Q-K5
10	QKt-B3 / QKt-Q2		KtxB / RPxKt	P-KKt4 / B-Kt3	QKt-B3 / P-KR3	Castles / QxR
11	Q-K2 / B-R4	P-QR3	BxP / PxB	P-KR4 / P-KR3	KtxBP / RxKt	Q-Kt3+
12	Q-Ksq / BxKt	KtxB / RPxKt	Q-B2 / K-B2	KtxB / PxKt	Kt-K5 / B-K5	
13	KtxKBP / Resigns (2)	Kt-Kt5+	Kt-B3 / Q-B2	BxPch / K-R2	BxP / B-Q4	
14			Kt-K5ch / K-Ktsq	P-Kt5+	KtxR / Q-KBsq	
15			QxP / B-Qsq		KtxRPch / K-Rsq	
16			B-B4 / Q-K2		Kt-B7ch / K-Ktsq	
17			B-Kt5 / Q-Ksq		Kt-Kt5ch / K-Rsq	
18			RxKt+		RxKt+	

(1) Threatens RxB.

(2) Correspondence Game between A E Blackmar and L S Atkinson.

NOTE.—The French Defence now often runs into the Blackmar Gambit, viz.: 1 P-K4 1 P-K3, 2 P-Q4 2 P-Q4, 3 P-QB3 3 PxP, 4 Kt-Q2 4 Kt-B3, 5 P-B3 5 PxP, 6 KKtxP. If 4 P-B3 4 B-Q3, 5 PxP (or Kt-Q2) 5 Q-R5ch+.

THE BLACKMAR GAMBIT.

	7	8	9	10	11

(See Diagram on page 84.)

	7	8	9	10	11
4	P-K3				
5	B-Q3 / Kt-KB3				
6	P-B3 / P-QKt3	B-Q3			
7	B-K3 / B-Kt2	Castles / Kt-B3			
8	QKt-Q2 / Kt-Q4	QKt-Q2 / Castles			
9	Q-K2 / Kt-Q2	Kt-Kt5 / P-KR3			
10	CastlesQR / B-K2	RxKt / PxR		QxR	PxKt
11	Kt-K4 / P-KR3	Kt-R7 / R-Ksq	P-KB4	QKt-K4 / Q-K2	Q-R5+
12	B-Q2! / KKt-B3	Q-R5 / B-Bsq (2)	Q-R5 / KxKt	Q-R5 / B-Q2 (6)	
13	KtxKt / BxKt	Kt-K4+ (3)	Kt-K4 / PxKt	Kt-R7 / KxKt (7)	
14	Kt-K5 / KtxKt		BxRP / PxB	Kt-B6ch / K-Rsq	
15	PxKt / B-Kt4		R-KBsq / Q-K2 (4)	BxP / P-KKt3 (8)	
16	K-Ktsq / BxB (1)		R-B3+ (5)		

(1) An unfinished Correspondence Game.

(2) If 12 Kt-K2, or B-K2, or B-B5, or B-K4, then 13 Kt-K4+.

(3) If 13 KxKt, 14 Kt-Kt5ch, or 14 KtxBPch. If 13 B-Kt2, 14 KKtxBPch+.

(4) If 15 Q-Q2, 16 B-Kt5ch, and then to B6+.

(5) If 16 P-Q7, 17 B-B4ch+. **If 16 P-K4, 17 R-Kt3.** If 16 P-B3, 17 BxRch+.

(6) If 12 PxKt, mate in two. If 12 P-KKt3, mate in four. (a)   If 12 P-KB3, 13 Q-Kt6+.

(7) If 13 P-KKt3, or KR-Qsq, 14 QKt-B6ch+.

(8) White mates in eight moves. (b)

(a) I cannot discover it.—E.M.

(b) There appears to be a mate in six moves, e.g.: 1 Q-R4 1 BxPch, 2 QxB 2 QxKt best, 3 B-Kt5ch 3 K-Kt2 best, 4 Q-R6ch 4 K-Ktsq, 5 BxQ, and mates next move.

THE BLACKMAR GAMBIT.

(See Diagram on page 84.)

	12	13	14	15	16
4	B-Kt5				
5	P-B3				
	Kt-KB3		P-K4		Kt-KB3
6	B-Q3		B-QB4	Q-R4ch (5)	B-Q3
	P-K3		P-K5	B-Q2	P-K3
7	Castles		BxBPch	Q-Kt3	Castles
	B-Q3		K-K2	P-K5	P-B3
8	Q-Ksq	QKt-Q2	BxKt	Kt-Kt5	QKt-Q2
	Castles	Castles	P-KR3 (4)	Q-B3	B-Q3
9	Q-R4	Q-Ksq	Q-K2	B-QB4	Q-Ksq
	BxKt	Kt-B3	BxKt	Kt-KR3	B-R4
10	RxB	Q-R4	PxB	R-Bsq+ (6)	Kt-K4
	QKt-Q2 (1)	P-KR3	RxB		B-Kt3
11	B-KKt5	Kt-K4	QxPch		KKt-Kt5
	P-KKt3	KtxKt	K-B2		B-K2
12	RxKt	QxB	QxKtP		KtxKtch (7)
	B-K2	P-KB4	Kt-Q2		PxKt
13·	RxKtPch	Q-R3	Q-Q5ch+		KtxKP
	BPxR	Q-B3			PxKt
14	BxB+ (2)	B-K3			B-QB4
		QR-Ksq			Castles
15		BxKt			B-R6
		PxB			R-Ksq
16		Kt-K5 (3)			QxPch
					K-Rsq
17					Q-Kt4
					B-Bsq (8)

(1) If 10 P-KR3, 11 BxRP+.

(2) Game, Blackmar and D Daponte.

(3) Thus far this is a Game between A E Blackmar and J A Galbreath. White played 16 Kt-Kt5, and Black played QxRch and lost. He should have played Q-Kt3.

(4) If 8 PxKt, 9 Q-Kt3+.

(5) Showing the purpose of White's fifth move.

(6) Game, Blackmar and L L Labatt.

(7) The position at this point is shown by the Diagram on next page.

(8) Correspondence Game between A E Blackmar and L S Atkinson, discontinued after the seventeenth move.

THE BLACKMAR GAMBIT.

1	P-Q4 / P-Q4	2	P-K4 / PxP	3	P-KB3 / PxP	4	KtxP / B-Kt5	5	P-B3 / Kt-KB3	6	B-Q3 / P-K3
7	Castles / P-B3	8	QKt-Q2 / B-Q3	9	Q-Ksq / B-R4	10	Kt-K4 / B-Kt3	11	KKt-Kt5 / B-K2	12	KtxKtch /

Position after White's 12th move.

BLACK.

WHITE.

	17	18	19	20
12	PxKt		BxKt	
13	KtxKP / PxKt		KtxKP / PxKt	
14	B-QB4 / Castles	B-B2	QxPch / B-K2	K-Bsq
15	B-R6 / R-Ksq	BxP / BxB	B-QKt5 / Q-Q2	B-KB4 / B-B2
16	QxPch / K-Rsq	QxB / Q-Q2	BxBch / PxB	B-Q6ch / K-Ktsq
17	Q-Kt4 / P-KB4	Q-K2 / R-Bsq	QxKtPch / K-Qsq	B-QB4 / Q-Q2
18	RxP / Q-Q2	Q-R5ch / R-B2	QxKtP / R-Ksq	RxB / PxR
19	QR-KBsq / B-Q3	R-B5 (2) / Q-K3	R-B7·+	QxP+
20	Q-Kt5+ (1)	B-Q2 (3)		

(1) If Black plays 20 B-K2, White mates in seven moves. (A) If 20 BxR, mate in two. If 20 Q-K2, 21 R-B8ch wins. If 20 Q-Qsq, 21 R-B7 21 R-Ktsq (21 Kt-Q2, 22 B-Kt7ch, mating in two), 22 B-Kt7ch wins.

(2) If 19 B-Kt5 19 Q-Q4.

(3) If 20 Kt-Q2, 21 P-Q5 21 PxP, 22 R-Ksq.

(A) Mate in five by 21 B-Kt7ch 21 KxB, 22 R-B7ch, &c.—E. M.

BLACKMAR'S SECOND GAMBIT.

1	2	3	4	5
P-Q4 P-KB4	P-K4 PxP	P-KB3 PxP	KtxP Kt-KB3	B-Q3 (1)

	1	2	3	4	5	6
5	P-K3	P-KKt3	P-Q3			
6	Kt-Kt5 P-KKt3	Kt-Kt5 P-Q4	P-KR3 Kt-B3			
7	KtxRP RxKt	KtxRP RxKt	Kt-Kt5 P-K4		P-KKt3	
8	BxPch R-B2	BxPch K-Q2	KtxRP P-K5		KtxP KtxKt	
9	B-Kt5 B-K2	BxR KtxB	BxP KtxB (5)		BxPch K-Q2	
10	Castles K-Bsq	Castles Q-Ksq	Q-R5ch K-K2		Q-R5 (6) B-Kt2 (7)	
11	BxR KxB	Q-B3 Kt-KB3	Castles Q-Ksq	B-K3	P-Q5 Kt-Q5 (8)	Kt-Bsq
12	BxKt BxB	Kt-B3 P-B3	B-Kt5ch KtxB	P-Q5 B-Ktsq	Q-Kt4ch P-K3	Q-Kt4ch P-K3
13	Q-R5ch K-Bsq (2)	B-B4 Q-Kt3	QxKtch K-Q2	B-Kt5ch KtxB	B-R7+	PxKtch PxP
14	Q-R8ch+ (3)	QR-Ksq (4)	KtxBch RxKt	QxKtch K-Q2		Castles+
15			QxPch+	KtxBch K-Bsq		
16				Q-Kt4ch K-Ktsq		
17				Kt-Q7ch K-Bsq		
18				R-B8+		

(1) The position is like that of the From Gambit, except that White has given KBP instead of QP, and is a move ahead. (A very material difference.— E.M.)

(2) If 13 K-K2, 14 RxB+.

(3) Game between A E Blackmar and A Labry.

(4) If 14 QxBP, 15 BxKt 15 RxB, 16 Q-R3ch 16 K-Qsq, 17 Q-R8+.

(5) If 9 Q-K2, 10 KtxKtch+.

(6) Appears better than B-B5ch, P-Q5, or Q-Kt4ch.

(7) If 10 P-K3, 11 P-Q5 11 Kt-K4, 12 PxPch 12 K moves, 13 BxKt+.

(8) If Kt goes to any other square, White mates in two.

THE MEADOW HAY AND STONEWALL OPENINGS.

THE "Meadow Hay" is an invention of Mr Preston Ware, of Boston. Its first move is P-QR4 for either attack or defence. Mr Steinitz gave it some passing attention in 1878, and pronounced its irregularity more manifest than its value, and said it was not likely to supercede the debuts of the middle Pawns, which free the actions of the Queens and Bishops. When it is remembered, he remarked, that there are actually over 400 different ways of starting the game on both sides, on the first move only, without proceeding further, it would occasion no surprise that originality is sometimes applied to the very first move, and strange Openings are thus introduced. Mr Ware has played the "Meadow Hay" at Chess Congresses in Europe and America, and proved it to possess considerable strength among the Irregular Openings.

The "Stonewall" Opening was also invented by Mr Ware, but thus far has attracted little attention.

Notes, to opposite page.

(1) And White mates in four moves. This game is one of a match played by Mr Ware with Mr Keyes, in Boston, in 1878. Mr Ware played his "Meadow Hay" Opening in all the ten games of the match, winning nine of them.

(2) Mr Steinitz would have preferred P-QKt3.

(3) Black's RP was bound to fall, and the open R file gives White the better position. The game is one won by Mr Ware from Capt Mackenzie.

(4) From a game won from Mr Ware by Capt Mackenzie.

(5) The "Stonewall" Opening.

(6) A loss of time. Mr Sellman recommends P-QKt4. From a game won by Mr Ware from Mr Weiss, at the Vienna International Chess Congress, 1882.

(7) Beginning a counter attack.

(8) A weak move. The game was won from Mr Ware by Mr Paulsen at the Vienna Congress, 1882.

THE MEADOW HAY OPENING.

	1	2	3
1	P-QR4 / P-K4		
2	P-QB3 / P-Q4	P-R5 / P-Q4	P-QB3 / P-KB4
3	P-Q4 / P-K5	P-K3 / P-KB4	P-Q4 / P-K5
4	B-B4 / B-Q3	P-R6 / PxP (2)	B-B4 / Kt-KB3
5	BxB / QxB	Kt-KB3 / P-K5	P-K3 / P-Q4
6	P-K3 / B-B4	Kt-K5 / Kt-KB3	Kt-KR3 / B-Q3
7	Q-B2 / Kt-KB3	P-Q4 / B-Q3	P-B4 / P-B3
8	Kt-Q2 / Castles	B-K2 / Castles	P-B5 / BxB
9	P-R3 / P-QR4	Castles / P-B4	KtxB / P-QKt3
10	P-KB4 / PxPen pass	P-QKt3 / B-K3	P-QKt4 / P-QR4
11	QxB / Q-Kt6ch	B-Kt2 / QKt-Q2	P-Kt5 / Castles
12	K-Qsq / PxP	RxP+ (3)	PxBP / KtxP
13	Kt-K2 / PxB(Q)ch		B-Kt5 / Kt-Kt5
14	KtxQ / Q-Kt3		Castles / Q-B2
15	Q-B4 / Q-Q6ch		P-B6 / P-Kt4
16	K-Ksq / Kt-R3		Kt-R5 / Kt-Kt5
17	R-KKtsq / Kt-K5		P-Kt3 / Q-B2+ (4)
18	Q-R6 / P-Kt3		
19	Kt-B4 / Q-B5 (1)		

THE STONEWALL OPENING.

	1	2
1	P-Q4 / P-Q4	Kt-KB3
2	P-KB4 (5) / P-K3	P-KB4 / P-KKt3
3	Kt-KB3 / Kt-KB3	Kt-KB3 / B-Kt2
4	P-K3 / B-Q3	P-K3 / P-Q3
5	B-Q3 / P-B4	B-K2 / Castles
6	P-B3 / Kt-B3	Castles / QKt-Q2
7	Castles / P-QR3	P-B4 / P-B3
8	B-Q2 / Castles	Kt-B3 / Q-B2
9	P-QR3 / P-QKt3	P-K4 / P-K4
10	P-R3 / B-Kt2	BPxP / PxP
11	B-Ksq / Kt-K5	PxP / P-Q5
12	QKt-Q2 / KtxKt	Kt-B4 / Q-Kt3 (7)
13	QxKt / Kt-R4	K-Rsq / Kt-Kt5
14	R-Qsq / Kt-B5	B-K2 / Kt-Q2
15	Q-K2 / Kt-R4 (6)	Q-Ksq / Q-Qsq
16	B-R4+	P-KR3 / KKt-B3
17		B-K3 / P-KR3
18		R-Qsq / R-Ksq
19		P-R3 (8) / PxP+

For Notes see opposite page.

MODERN CHESS OPENINGS.

A compilation of the most popular Openings, with the latest variations.

——:o:——

Orders, or suggestions in reference to the work (which will be of a similar character to the " Synopsis of the Chess Openings ") to be addressed to the Publisher, W W Morgan Jun., Office of THE CHESS PLAYER'S CHRONICLE, 17 Medina Road, Holloway, London, N.

THE STAUNTON CHESSMEN.

The following are the opinions expressed upon the STAUNTON CHESSMEN *by the leading journals of the day :*

" A set of Chessmen of a pattern combining elegance and solidity to a degree hitherto unknown, has recently appeared under the auspices of the celebrated player, Mr. STAUNTON. A guiding principle has been to give by their form a signification to the various Pieces—thus the King is represented by a crown, the Queen by a coronet, &c. The Pieces generally are fashioned with convenience to the hand ; and it is to be remarked that while there is so great an accession to elegance of form, it is not attained at the expense of practical utility · Mr. STAUNTON's pattern adopts but elevates the conventional form ; and the base of the Pieces being of a large diameter, they are more steady than in ordinary sets."—*Times.*

" A new set of Chessmen has recently appeared under the auspices of Mr. STAUNTON, who, observing their manifest superiority over the old figures in ordinary use, not only as works of art, but in the more practical necessities of convenience, has vouchsafed the guarantee of his name and recommendation. Those who have been in the habit of playing the game will remember the awkward and inelegant structure of the generality of the shapes which have been in vogue. No artistic feeling until now has ever been brought to bear upon the formation of a pattern which should satisfy the eye both on the score of elegance and propriety." . . —*Standard.*

No.		£	s	d
000	Ebony and Boxwood, in polished Mahogany box, velvet lined · · · ·	0	15	0
	Base of King, 1¾ in. diameter.			
00	Ebony and Boxwood, large size, in polished Mahogany box, velvet lined · · ·	0	17	6
	Base of King, 1½ in. diameter.			
0	Ebony and Boxwood, loaded with lead, superior finished, in Mahogany case · ·	1	5	0
	Base of King, 1¾ in. diameter.			
1	Ebony and Boxwood, loaded with lead, in ornamental Cartonpierre Casket · ·	1	15	0
	Base of King, 1¾ in. diameter			
1½	Ebony and Boxwood, loaded with lead, small size Club, in Mahogany case ·	1	15	0
	Base of King, 1½ in. diameter.			
2	Ebony and Boxwood, loaded with lead, Club size, in strong Mahogany case · ·	2	5	0
	Base of King, 2 in. diameter.			
3	Finest African Ivory, in Cartonpierre Casket · · · · ·	4	0	0
	Base of King, 1¾ in. diameter.			
4	Finest African Ivory, in Cartonpierre Casket, richly lined · · · ·	6	0	0
	Base of King, 1¾ in. diameter.			
4½	Finest African Ivory, small size Club, in Cartonpierre Casket, richly lined ·	8	0	0
	Base of King, 1½ in. diameter.			
5	Finest African Ivory, Club size, in extra large Cartonpierre Casket, richly lined ·	10	0	0
	Base of King, 2 in. diameter.			
5	In handsome Spanish Mahogany case, fitted in trays with divisions, lined throughout with rich silk velvet · · · · · · · · · · ·	11	5	0

Nos. 3, 4, 4½, 5, may be had in velvet-lined polished Walnut cases, with locks, at same price.

In order to guard against fraudulent and inferior imitations of the STAUNTON CHESSMEN, the public are requested to observe that each box bears the signature of Mr. Staunton.

THE STAUNTON CHESS-BOARD,

Folding Leather, richly ornamented ; in Cartonpierre, to match the Staunton Caskets.   Price £2 10s.

— :0: —

FOLDING LEATHER CHESS BOARDS, with red and buff squares, suitable for the Staunton Chessmen.

16 in., 6s; 18 in., 7s 6d; 20 in., 9s 9d; 22 in., 12s.

W. W. MORGAN Jun., 17 MEDINA ROAD, HOLLOWAY, LONDON, N.

THE
IN STATU QUO CHESS BOARD.

This invention supplies a want felt by all Chess players. The IN STATU QUO Chess-board is so contrived that the Game may at any time be discontinued, and the board folded and placed in its Case without the Chessmen being disturbed. For ordinary play, as well as for sea or railway use, this Board has obvious advantages not possessed by any other hitherto offered to the public.

PRICES.

	£	s	d
9 inch polished mahogany board, with bone men complete, in leather case	£1	10	0
Ditto, enclosed in leather lock case, book shape, with brass bolts to prevent the board closing when in use, with men complete	1	15	0
Ditto, with division on the board for the captured Pieces, enclosed in leather lock case, with bolts, &c., and men complete	2	0	0

Any of the above, with **Ivory** Chessmen, 15s per set **extra**.

	£	s	d
13 inch polished mahogany board, with extra large size men, enclosed in leather lock case	2	10	0
Ditto, with division on the board for captured Pieces, enclosed in leather lock case, with bolts, &c.	3	15	0

Either of the above, with **Ivory** Chessmen, 20s per set extra.

RAILWAY CHESS BOARD.—Polished mahogany, folding, with pegged men, complete, 5in, 6s 6d; 6in, 7s 6d; 8in, 10s; 10in, 12s; 12in, 15s 6d; 14in, £1 5s.

STUDENT'S CHESS BOARD.—Leather, in case, with pegged men, complete, 6inch, 5s; 7in, 6s; 8in, 7s.

WHITTINGTON CHESS BOARD.—Polished Mahogany, with folding flaps and pegged men, complete, 8in, 14s; 12in, £1 8s.

STAUNTON CHESSMEN.—(For full particulars see last page.) 15s, 17s 6d, £1 5s, £1 15s, £2 5s, £4, £6, £8, £10 and £11 5s per set.

ENGLISH PATTERN CHESSMEN.—Rosewood and boxwood, 1s 6d, 2s, 2s 6d, 3s, 3s 9d, 4s 6d, 5s 6d, 6s 9d and 8s 6d per set. Ebony and boxwood, superior quality, French polished, 4s, 5s, 7s 6d, 10s 6d, 15s and 18s 6d per set.

EDINBORO' CLUB PATTERN CHESSMEN.—Ebony and boxwood, French polished, 10s, 12s 6d, 15s and 18s 6d per set. Solid Ivory, in best box, £3 7s 6d per set.

DUBLIN PATTERN CHESSMEN.—Ebony and boxwood, French polished, 10s, 12s 6d, 15s and 18s 6d per set.

ST. GEORGE'S CLUB PATTERN CHESSMEN.—Ebony and boxwood, French polished, £1 5s, ditto, loaded, £1 10s, ditto, ditto, largest size, £1 16s per set.

BONE CHESSMEN.—3s, 4s, 5s, 7s, 8s 6d and 10s per set; handsomely carved, 15s 6d and £1 1s per set; improved pattern, solid bone, 7s 6d, 10s 6d and 15s 6d per set.

CHESS BOARDS.

MAHOGANY.

Polished rosewood and holly squares.	16in s d	18in s d	20in s d	22in s d	24in s d
Superior quality	8 0	10 6	12 6	—	—
Best quality	16 0	19 0	22 0	25 0	28 0

ROSEWOOD. Best polished Club Boards, 24 inch, £1 16s each.

FOLDING LEATHER BOARDS.

	10in s d	12in s d	14in s d	16in s d	18in s d	20in s d	22in s d
Black and White squares.							
Ordinary quality, on wood	1 6	1 9	2 0	2 3	3 6	4 6	—
Superior quality, on wood	1 9	2 3	2 6	3 0	4 0	5 3	—
Best quality, on millboard	3 0	3 6	4 3	4 9	6 0	8 6	9 6
Red and White squares.							
Ordinary quality, on wood	1 9	2 3	2 6	3 0	4 0	5 3	—
Superior quality, on wood	2 3	2 6	3 0	3 6	4 9	6 6	—
Best quality, on millboard	3 9	4 6	5 3	6 0	7 6	9 9	12 0

DRAUGHTSMEN.—Wood, 9d and 1s per set, hardwood, 1s, 1s 3d and 1s 6d per set; ebony and boxwood, ivory pattern, polished, 1s 6d, 2s and 2s 6d per set; ditto, best quality, polished, 3s, 3s 6d and 4s per set; ebony and boxwood, ditto, turned edge, 3s 6d, 4s and 4s 6d per set; bone draughtsmen, 5s, 6s 6d and 8s 6d per set; ivory draughtsmen, £1 7s, £1 11s 6d and £2 2s per set.—W W Morgan Jun., 17 Medina Road, Holloway, London, N.

SPECIAL BARGAIN.

——:o:——

VOLS. VI. VII. VIII.

OF THE

WESTMINSTER PAPERS,

TEN SHILLINGS AND SIXPENCE.

Neatly bound in three volumes, as good as new. Sent to any part of the United Kingdom, on receipt of 11s 6D.

——:o:——

SINGLE VOLUMES,—(VI, VII, VIII.)

FOUR SHILLINGS EACH.

Sent, carriage paid, to any part of the United Kingdom, on receipt of 4s 6D.

——:o:——

The three volumes contain upwards of five hundred and forty Problems; three hundred and thirty Games, annotated by John Wisker, J H Zukertort, and others; the Chess News of the time (May 1873 to April 1876 inclusive); Chess Articles, Analyses, &c.; Whist; Dramatic Notes, &c., &c.

W W MORGAN JUN., 17 Medina Road, Holloway, London, N.

GAMES OF THE MATCH

BETWEEN

STEINITZ & BLACKBURNE,

Played at the West End Chess Club, London, February-March 1876.

ANNOTATED BY W STEINITZ. PRICE ONE SHILLING,

Post free from W W Morgan jun., 17 Medina Road, Holloway, London, N

CATALOGUE OF BOOKS

ON THE

GAME OF CHESS

OFFERED FOR SALE BY

W W Morgan, Jun., 17 Medina Road, Holloway, London, N.

————:o:————:o:————

An easy introduction to the Game of Chess: containing one hundred examples of Games, and a great variety of critical situations and conclusions; including the whole of Philidor's analysis, with copious selections from Stamma, the Calabrois, &c. Arranged on a new plan, with instructions for learners, rendering a complete knowledge of that scientific Game perfectly easy of attainment. To which are added, Caissa: a Poem, by Sir William Jones; the Morals of Chess, by Dr Franklin; Chess and Whist compared; Anecdotes respecting Chess and Chess-Players, &c. 4s. 1809

The same book. A new edition. 4s. 1816

An introduction to the history and study of Chess; with copious descriptions, etymological and practical: together with a system of elementary rules for playing: to which is added, the analysis of Chess of André Danican Philidor. The whole simplifyed, and arranged in a manner entirely new, by an Amateur. **7s.** Cheltenham, 1804

Automaton. An attempt to analyse the Automaton Chess Player, of Mr De Kempelen. With an easy method of imitating the movements of that celebrated figure. Illustrated by original drawings. To which is added, a copious collection of the Knight's moves over the Chess board. 10s 6d. 1821

Automaton. A selection of fifty Games, from those played by the Automaton Chess-Player, during its exhibition in London, in 1820. 5s. 1820

("A complete analysis of the Pawn and Move Game, the Automaton invariably giving KBP and Move.")

Chess. Containing all the principal Openings and endings of Games, with selected Problems and illustrative moves. (Chambers's useful hand-book series). 1s. N.D.

Chess exemplified in a concise and easy notation, greatly facilitating practice. Being an introduction to the Game, on a system of progressive instruction and examples. By the late President of a select Chess Club. 5s. 1842

Crawley, Captain. Chess: its theory and practice; to which **is added a chapter on** Draughts. 2s 6d. N.D.

Dal Rio, Dr Ercole. The incomparable Game of Chess, developed after a new method of the greatest facility, from the first elements to the most scientific artifices of the Game. Translated from the Italian by J S Bingham, Esq. To which is prefixed, an essay on the origin of the Game, by Eyles Irwin, Esq. 7s 6d. 1820

Damiano, Ruy Lopez, and Salvio, on the Game of Chess; translated and arranged with remarks, observations, and copious notes on the games. Containing, also, several original games and situations, by the editor. To which are added, the elements of the Art of Playing without seeing the board. By J H Sarratt. 7s. 1813

Forbes, Duncan. The History of Chess, from the time of the early invention of the Game in India, till the period of its establishment in Western and Central Europe. 15s. 1860

Gianutio, and Gustavus Selenus, on the Game of Chess. Translated and arranged by J H Sarratt. 8s. 1817

Healey, F. A collection of two hundred Chess Problems. Including the Problems to which the prizes were awarded by the committees of the Era, the Manchester, the Birmingham, and the Bristol Chess Problem Tournaments. Accompanied by solutions. 30s. 1866

Jaenisch. A complete translation **(in two** volumes) of the celebrated Analysis **of the** Openings of the **Game of** Chess, **published** at St. Petersburg **in 1843.** By **C F De** Jaenisch, the great Russian player, Major (in the Engineering Department) in the Russian army; formerly assistant-professor of the science of mechanics at the Institute of the "ways of communication in Russia;" author of "Principles of equilibrium **and** motion" (published in the Russian language); also of "discoveries concerning the Chess-Knight," Knight of St. Anne (third class and of St. Stanislas (third class), etc. Vol. I. 21s. Cambridge, 1855-6

Catalogue of Chess Books for sale by W W Morgan Jun., continued.

Kenny, W S. Practical Chess Exercises; intended as a sequel to the Practical Chess Grammar; containing various Openings, Games, and Situations, with instructions and remarks on the principal moves of each party; for the use of those who have already a knowledge of the game. 4s 6d. 1818
The same book. Second Edition. 4s 6d. 1818

Kenny, W S. Practical Chess Grammar: or, an introduction to the Royal Game of Chess: in a series of plates. Designed to amuse and instruct the learner, remove the difficulties of this elegant and scientific Game, and render it attainable by the lowest capacity. 15s. 1817
The same book. Third edition, considerably improved. 15s. 1818

Kling. The Chess Euclid; a collection of two hundred Chess Problems and End-games. Composed by Herr Kling. Revised and corrected by the Author. 30s. 1849

Lambe, R. The History of Chess, together with short and plain instructions by which any one may easily play at it without the help of a teacher. 15s. 1764

Leitfaden fur Schachspieler verfasst von herausgeber des Bilguer'schen Schachhandbuchs. Dritte verbesserte auflage. 10s 6d. Leipzig, 1862

Le Jeu des Echecs. 5s. Amsterdam, 1792

Lewis, W. A selection of Games at Chess, played at the Westminster Chess Club, between Monsieur L C de la Bourdonnais and an English Amateur of first rate skill. 10s. 1835

Lewis, W. A series of progressive lessons on the Game of Chess, containing numerous general rules and remarks: also, the most approved method of beginning the Game exemplified in five Openings. With reasons for every move. The whole written expressly for the use of beginners. 10s 6d. 1831
The same book. Second edition. 10s 6d. 1833

Lewis, W. Chess for beginners. In a series of progressive lessons. Showing the most approved methods of beginning and ending the Game. With various situations and checkmates, illustrated by numerous diagrams, printed in colours. Second edition, revised and corrected. 5s. 1837
The same book. Third edition, revised and corrected. 5s. 1846

Lewis, W. Chess Problems. Being a selection of original positions; to which are added others, extracted from rare and valuable works, forming together one hundred ends of Games; won or drawn by brilliant and scientific moves; to which are added the names of the authors. 10s 6d. 1827

Lewis, William. Elements of the Game of Chess, or a new method of instruction in that celebrated Game, founded on scientific principles: containing numerous general rules, remarks and examples, by means of which, considerable skill in the Game may be acquired, in a comparatively short time. The whole written expressly for the use of beginners. 6s. 1822

Lewis, W. Fifty Games at Chess, which have actually been played, most of which occurred between the author and some of the best players in England, France, and Germany; to which is added some account of the village of Stroebeck, in Germany, with three Games played according to the method practised there. 9s. 1832

Lewis, W. The Chess-board companion: containing the laws of the Game; the value and power of the Pieces; remarks on the most approved methods of beginning the Game; with numerous examples, &c.; written expressly for the use of beginners. To which are added, several instructive Problems on Diagrams. **Seventh** edition. 2s 6d. N.D.
The same book. Ninth edition. 2s 6d. N.D.

Lewis, W. The Games of the match at Chess played by the London and the Edinburgh Chess Clubs, between the years 1824 and 1828, with numerous variations and remarks. 7s 6d. 1828

Lowenthal. A selection from the Problems of the Era Problem Tournament. With a preface by Herr Lowenthal. 10s 6s. 1857

Ludus Scacchiæ: Chesse-play. A Game, both pleasant, wittie, and politicke. with certain briefe instructions thereunto belonging; translated out of the Italian into the English tongue. Containing also therein, a prety and pleasant Poeme of a whole game played at Chesse. Written by G B. 15s. (Reprint of the original edition, dated) 1597

Moore, Thos D S. 100 Gems of Chess, selected from the Chess department of the Western Advertiser, of London, Ontario, published during 1872. 2s 6d. N.D.

Neumann, G R. Die Grundregeln des Schachspiels mit Erlauterungen. 2s 6d. Berlin, 1867

Philidor, A D. Analysis of the Game of Chess, illustrated by diagrams, on which are marked the situation of the party for the back-games and ends of parties: with critical remarks and notes by the author of the Stratagems of Chess. Translated from the last French edition, and further illustrated with notes, by W S Kenny. 6s. 1819

Pohlman, J G. Chess rendered familiar by tabular demonstrations of the various positions and movements, as described by Philidor. With many other critical situations and moves, and a concise introduction to the Game. 12s. 1819

Ponziani. Il Giuoco incomparabile degli Scacchi sviluppato con nuovo metodo per condurre chiunque colla Maggior facilità dai primi elementi sino alle finezze piu magistrali. Prima edizione Veneziana eseguita sopra quella di Modena del 1782 ridotta a moderna lezione ed arricchita di molte annotazioni e di otto tavole dietro la scorta delle Opere piu recenti, per Cura di Giusto Adolfo Co. Van-axel Castelli. 15s. Venezia, 1861

Preti, Jean. Traité complet, théorique et pratique sur les fins de parties au Jeu des Echecs. Illustré de trois cent quarante diagrammes. 10s. Paris, 1858

Sarratt, J H. A new treatise on the Game of Chess, on a plan of progressive improvement, hitherto unattempted ; containing a very considerable number of general rules, explanations, notes and examples : the object of these rules, &c. is to enable unpractised players to avoid crowded Games, to bring their Pieces into action speedily and properly, to become well acquainted with the Board, and gradually to comprehend and overcome the difficulties of this scientifick Game : and examples of intricate combination, illustrated by Games and Positions, teaching both attack and defence ; and adapted to the higher classes of players : concluding with a selection of unpublished Games, chiefly Gambits ; analysed with great care ; and including many remarkable situations, equally instructive and interesting. 5s. 1821

Souvenir of the Bristol Chess Club ; containing one hundred original Games of Chess, recently played, either between the best players in that society, or by them with other celebrated players of the day. With copious notes. 10s 6d. 1845

Stamma, Phillip. The noble Game of Chess ; or, a new and easy method to learn to play well in a short time : together with a curious account of its antiquity, derivation of its terms, &c. 21s. 1745

Studies of Chess : containing Caissa, a Poem, by Sir William Jones ; a systematic introduction to the Game ; and the whole analysis of Chess, by Mr A D Philidor. With original critical remarks, and compendious diagrams. A new edition,—in two volumes. 15s. 1850

Taylor, J Paul. Elementary Chess Problems. A selection from the compositions of J Paul Taylor. Containing fifty two-move Problems, and a few specimens of three-movers, &c., also some hints to composers of two-movers. 5s. 1880

The Accomplished Chess-Player ; An elementary treatise : with the Morals of Chess, by Dr Franklin. Third edition (Causton) 2s. N.D.

The Pocket Chess Board ; peculiarly adapted for Problems and transmission by Book post. 2s 6d.

Tomlinson, Charles. The Chess-Player's Annual for the year 1856. 10s 6d. 1856

Vielle, C. Méthode pour apprendre seul la marche des Echecs et la règle de ce jeu. 7s 6d. Paris, N.D.

Walker, George. A new treatise on Chess : containing the rudiments of the science, with an analysis of the best methods of playing the different Openings and ends of Games ; including many original positions, and a selection of fifty Chess Problems never before printed in this country. 12s. 1832
The same book. Second edition. 12s. 1833
The same book. Third edition. 12s. 1841

Walker, George. Chess made easy ; being a new introduction to the rudiments of that scientific and popular game. 7s. 1836
The same book New edition. 7s. 1850

Walker, George. The Philidorian ; a magazine of Chess, and other scientific Games. Complete in one volume. 21s. 1838

The above prices are for cash with order, and include postage to any part of the World.

Terms for hire of Chess Works, upon application.

Complete catalogue (from which above is an extract) sent free upon application Chess Books and Magazines, ancient or modern, procured to order.

—:o:—

W W MORGAN Jun.,

Dealer in **Chess Men,** Chess **Boards, Books,** and every requisite for the Game, Office of " The Chess Player's Chronicle," 17 Medina Road, Holloway, London, N.

THE
BRITISH CHESS MAGAZINE.
EDITED BY JOHN WATKINSON,
WITH THE CO-OPERATION OF

REV C E RANKEN,	J G CUNNINGHAM,	J PIERCE, M.A.,
REV W WAYTE,	E FREEBOROUGH,	W T PIERCE,
H J C ANDREWS,	T LONG, B.A.,	A E STUDD.

Annual subscription, 6s in advance, post free to all parts of the world. Single copies, 8d.

Orders for the Magazine, contributions of Games, Chess News, &c., and copies of exchanges, should be sent to John Watkinson, Fairfield, Huddersfield. P. O. Orders payable at Huddersfield. Solutions of Problems and all other matter connected with the Problem Department to H J C Andrews, The Chesnuts, Park End, Sydenham, Kent.

HUDDERSFIELD : J E WHEATLEY & CO., NEW STREET.

LONDON : TRUBNER & CO., LUDGATE HILL, E.C. NEW YORK : BRENTANO, 5 UNION SQUARE.

INDIA RUBBER
DIAGRAM FORMS.

BLACK.

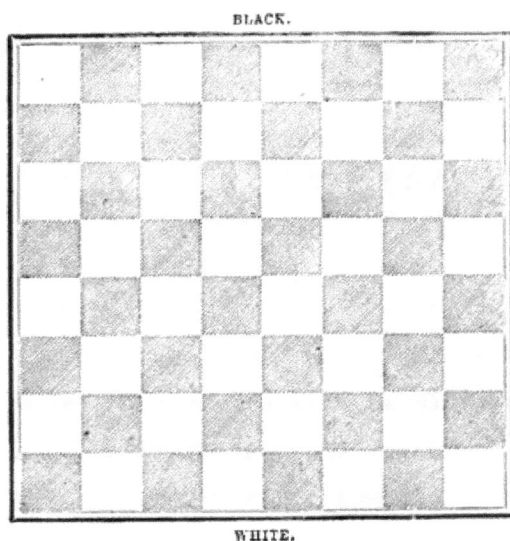

WHITE.

For printing Chess Diagrams, in size and form of above Diagram. Complete, in box, with ink, pad, &c., 10s. ; sent, carriage free to any address in the Kingdom, on receipt of remittance, by W W Morgan jun., 17 Medina Road, Holloway, N.

INDIA RUBBER CHESS TYPE.

For printing Problems, Positions, &c., on Diagram Forms (size and form as above). Complete, in box, with ink, pad, &c., 4s. per set ; sent, carriage free to any address the Kingdom, on receipt of remittance, by W W Morgan jun., 17 Medina Road, Holloway, London, N.

Loose Diagram Forms (same size Diagram as above), 1s 1d per 50, post free.

Diagram Books, with counterpart for Solutions, numbered and perforated. 1s 1d.

THE

Chess Player's Chronicle,

JOURNAL OF INDOOR AND OUTDOOR AMUSEMENTS.

—:o:—

PUBLISHED EVERY WEDNESDAY, PRICE 3D.

3s 3d per quarter, 13s per annum, post free if paid in advance.

Special terms to Clubs or others, requiring a number of copies each week.

SPECIMENS FREE, UPON APPLICATION.

All communications, remittances or orders to be addressed to the Proprietor, W W Morgan Jun., 17 Medina Road, Holloway, London, N.

THE CHESS OPENINGS. By R B Wormald. Second edition. 7s 6d.

POSITIONS IN THE CHESS OPENINGS. By T Long. 7s 6d.

WAIFS AND STRAYS. By Capt H A Kennedy. Second edition. 5s.

GAMES. Gossip and others. (Book I of Morgan's Shilling Chess Library.) 1s.

Special offer.—The numbers of THE CHESS PLAYER'S CHRONICLE, January 1878 to June 1885, seven yearly volumes, sent carriage free to any address in Europe or America, on receipt of 21s. Single volumes, 1878 to 1882 inclusive, 3s each; 1883-4, 5s; 1884-5, 5s.

London International Tournament of 1883.—The second edition of the book of the Games played in this Tournament is now ready. With an index of Openings, by H E Bird. 15s.

Any of the above sent, carriage paid, upon receipt of remittance, payable to W W Morgan Jun., 17 Medina Road, Holloway, London, N.

—:o:—

W W MORGAN Jun.,
PRINTER, PUBLISHER, STATIONER, &c.

Dealer in Chess Men, Chess Boards, Books, Playing Cards, and every requisite for Games. Wholesale and Retail. 10 per cent discount to Clubs.

—:o:—

Exceptional facilities for Chess literature.
Contracts entered into for the Printing and Publishing of Works on the Game.
Special terms arranged with authors for the production of new Books.

www.ingramcontent.com/pod-product-compliance
Lightning Source LLC
Chambersburg PA
CBHW032356280326
41935CB00008B/592